Haynes
eBay
Manual

© Haynes Publishing 2005

Published by: Haynes Publishing
Sparkford, Yeovil, Somerset BA22 7JJ
Tel: 01063 442030 Fax: 01963 440001
Int. tel: +44 1963 442030 Fax: +44 1963 440001
E-mail: sales@haynes.co.uk
Web site: www.haynes.co.uk

British Library Cataloguing in Publication Data:
A catalogue record for this book is available from the British Library

ISBN 1 84425 219 1

Printed in Britain by J. H. Haynes & Co. Ltd, Sparkford

Haynes

eBay
Manual

The indispensable step-by-step
guide to the world's leading
online marketplace

Haynes Publishing

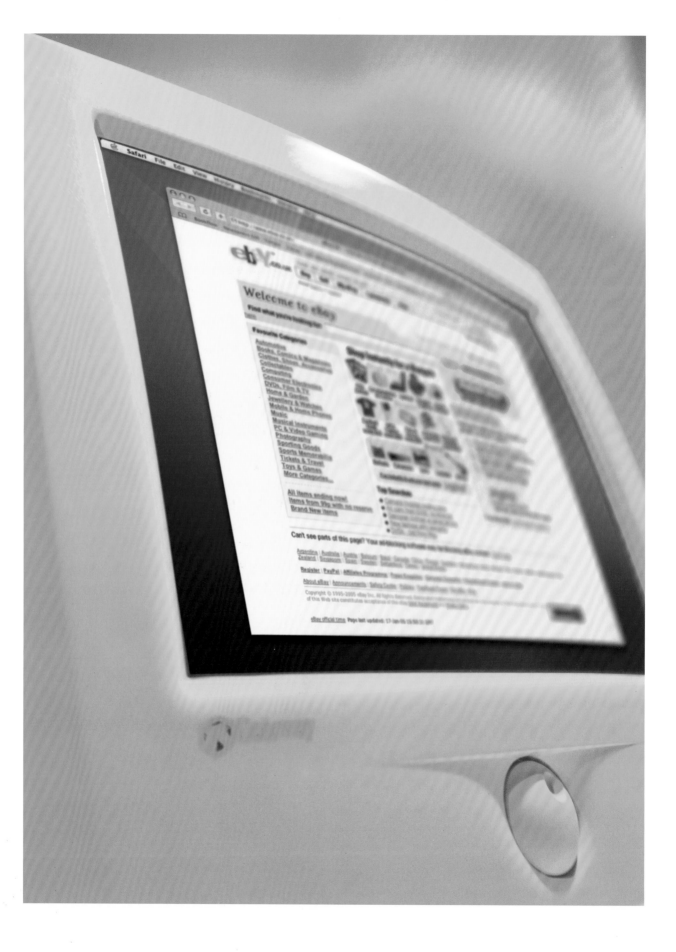

Contents

Introduction

Self-billed as 'the world's online marketplace', eBay is unquestionably successful. Staggeringly so, in fact. Founded in September 1995, eBay has (as of late 2004) 114 million registered users worldwide trading in more than 50,000 categories.

Almost half a million people in the US make at least a part-time living from selling on eBay. Many of them do very nicely indeed on a full-time basis. At any given time, there are more than 20 million items available on eBay worldwide, with more than 3.5 million new items added each day. A car sells every four minutes and a CD every 11 seconds. Globally, goods worth around $30 billion traded through eBay in 2004 alone.

Impressive numbers these may be, and numbers that are growing all the time – but they're *just* numbers. How does eBay relate to you if you have a hankering to buy and sell?

eBay appreciates your business – and in time you'll come to appreciate eBay.

Easy steps

To the newcomer, the truth is that eBay is a bit of a minefield. Indeed, it's hard to understand just how such a complex website came to so dominate the once-competitive field of internet auctions. At times during the writing of this book, we were left thinking it a miracle that anybody ever worked out how to use it at all!

But dominate it did, and still does. If you have something to sell or are looking for a bargain, eBay is undisputedly the place to be. You see, the other truth about eBay is that it's fun. Addictively so, in fact. It can also be highly profitable or simply a good outlet for stuff you no longer need but can't bear to throw out. Almost anything has a value to somebody on eBay. We wouldn't have written this book if we didn't honestly believe that learning how to trade on eBay is worth the effort.

A couple of cautionary comments ...

First, making a successful purchase or a sale on eBay is 'hard'. It requires effort and understanding. eBay is neither a shop nor an auction house, but rather a marketplace where people come together to buy and sell. It's a marketplace with rules and procedures, of course, some of which are complex, but it's also a marketplace that lacks some of the security of the high street. If you are nervous about trading directly with people outside the highly regulated framework of consumer legislation, you might not find eBay to your taste. That would be a shame, because the overwhelming majority of eBay transactions are smooth and successful, but trading on eBay is simply not the same as buying goods over the counter. It's important to take that on board.

Secondly, eBay is evolving. In fact, it's forever launching revamped web page designs, search tools for buyers and new ways of showcasing items for sellers. Whatever we write today may well have changed by tomorrow, and you'll doubtless find that some eBay pages look different from the screenshots on these page.

However, unless eBay reinvents itself completely overnight, we're confident that this book will teach you everything you need to know in order to get started. That's a tall order for a slim volume but we're confident that you'll soon be reaping the rewards.

And if not ... well, you can always flog it on eBay and get your own back.

We have blurred User IDs and other personal information throughout this manual to protect the privacy of those who trade on eBay.

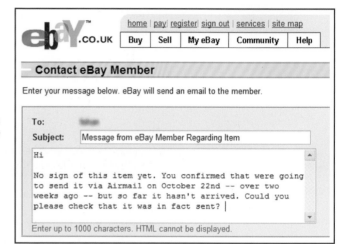

Although there are some measures in place to resolve disputes, eBay works primarily on the basis of direct contact between the buyer and the seller. In other words, if you have a problem, you should be prepared to work it out yourself.

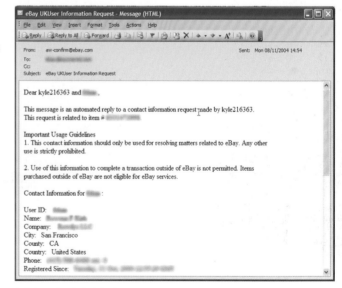

Ask for a trader's telephone number and you shall receive (so long as you are currently engaged in a transaction or have been so recently).

1

PART **1**

eBay MANUAL
Live auctions vs eBay

PART **1**

Live auctions explored

A normal, real-life, live auction held in an auction room and conducted by a trained auctioneer is one thing; an internet auction is something else entirely. The distinction is more than one of location or medium alone. As well as obvious dissimilarities in location and medium, the bidding and buying processes on an internet auction operate along substantially different lines. These distinctions are not immediately apparent from the outside looking in but become critical the moment you want to participate in – or win – an internet auction.

Story of a wardrobe

Let's say you go to an auction house hoping to buy a wardrobe. The auctioneer opens the bidding at £10. Like virtually everybody else in the room, you sit on your hands and wait for somebody else to make the first move. You figure the wardrobe is easily worth £20, perhaps £25. Eventually, somebody bids £10. The auction is underway.

A second bidder now enters the fledgling fray and waves their card in the air. '£11 to the bidder in the corner,' proclaims the auctioneer.

A few seconds of inactivity follow while the auctioneer scans the room. Seizing the moment, you wave your bid card and catch his eye. 'Twelve pounds,' comes the acknowledgement.

So what's just happened here? Some factors to note.

● The auctioneer determines the bid increment, or the difference between one bid and the next. In this case, each new bid raises the price of the wardrobe by one pound. You know exactly where you stand at each moment and know exactly how much you'll have to pay if you make a bid and win the auction.

● It's simply not possible to place a losing bid. That is, if the auction currently stands at £12, you can't bid £11. Patently obvious though this sounds, it's an important distinction to remember as you read on.

● You could conceivably shortcut the auction by bidding way over the odds early on: '£50 for the wardrobe!' The chance are that nobody will bid against you and you'll win the item. But the chances are also that you'll pay much, much more than the wardrobe would have fetched through incremental bidding. Bidding high and early is not a particularly smart tactic unless you're loaded and determined to get the item at any price.

● The moment you place a bid, you automatically become the auction leader. There is no room for doubt here. Moreover, everybody else knows that you are the highest bidder and knows exactly how much you have bid. They don't know how far you are prepared to go, of course, but a live auction is essentially 'open' in a way that internet auctions are not, as we shall see.

Up, up and away

Let's return to our auction scenario. You have just bid £12 and currently stand to win the wardrobe. But somebody else chips in with a £13 bid. You are now completely out of the running. You have, as a matter of certainty, just lost the wardrobe. All you can do to rejoin the game is place another bid. Let's say you bid £14 – and get immediately topped again. This bid/counter-bid process may now continue for several minutes, with the wardrobe price creeping upwards one pound at a time: £15, £16, £17, etc. The important thing to remember is that there is no ceiling on the auction: it will close and the wardrobe will sell when, and only when, all other bidders give up and leave the last bid unchallenged.

Let's imagine that the price eventually reaches £25 in somebody else's favour. This is the top price that you were prepared to pay for the wardrobe a few minutes ago. But is it *still* your top price? Have you been caught up in the thrill of the chase? Perhaps, you tell yourself, you should make one final bid. After all, the bid increment is only £1 and having come this far you'll be almost as happy to pay £26 for the wardrobe as £25.

So perhaps you bid £26. If your opponent outbids you yet again, you go through the same thought-process. Is the wardrobe now 'worth' £28? In the excitement of the moment, how high are you really prepared to go? Do you even know? Remember, there's no time limit here: you can keep bidding as long as you like. If you stop bidding now, will you kick yourself later? After all, you still have to find a wardrobe somewhere, and that extra couple of pounds would have saved you a lot of bother.

"TRYING TO AUCTION ME WON'T WORK!"

Pile on the pressure

Let's assume that your first opponent does in fact throw in the towel when you bid £26. The wardrobe, it seems, is yours. Then suddenly, seconds before the auctioneer wields the hammer to secure the sale, a new bidder chips in with £27. What to do? If you bid £28, you risk being drawn into another bidding war; if you give up now, you risk losing the wardrobe for the sake of £2.

The auctioneer throws you a quizzical glance, but he's getting impatient. There's no time to consider the matter further ... you must put up now or walk away ...

This new bidder has played the game well (for a game it is). By monitoring the auction dispassionately rather than as an active participant and by refusing to show his hand until the very end, the pressure is suddenly on you to make a snap decision. However – and this is an absolutely critical point – you do have the option to place a higher bid if you want to. No matter how late the new bidder comes in, it's never too late for you to indicate to the auctioneer that you're not done yet. In other words, the auction is not over until *you* say it's over.

PART 1

The eBay difference

The great mystery, fun and frustration with any live auction is that nobody knows when it will end. Not where, but when. An auction ends when only one party is left in the contest but timing plays no important factor in this. This is a crucial distinction between live auctions and eBay, and one that it's important to take on board at the outset.

An eBay auction ends at a set time and the winning bid is the highest bid at that time. When you take part in an eBay auction, it really doesn't matter what price you are prepared to pay: all that matters is that you happen to be in the lead when the auction closes. If somebody else outbids you at the death, too bad. There's no way of raising your bid after the final whistle, no chance of delaying the auctioneer's hammer, and no second chances.

Here are three possible strategies for dealing with the extra dynamic of a fixed-period.

Timing is all, on eBay.

Current bid:	**£15.00**
	[Place Bid >]
Time left:	**35 mins 49 secs** 7-day listing Ends 30-Nov-04 09:01:43 GMT
Start time:	23-Nov-04 09:01:43 GMT

www.CartoonStock.com

1. Bid early

It's tempting to place a bid early in an eBay auction and then effectively forget about it. Many people do just this, and there's no question that a high opening bid will put off much of the potential competition. But the trouble is twofold.

On one hand, just like shouting '£50 for the wardrobe!', you risk paying well over the odds. If only one other bidder would have been prepared to go as high as £27, why pay almost double when you don't have to? Of course, this is hypothetical: you'll never know where the auction would have stopped if you hadn't placed an early high bid.

On the other hand, it's simply not possible to make a high bid in the normal sense. For instance, if the starting price for a wardrobe is £10, you can bid £50 – but your bid will show up on eBay as £11 and nobody will know how high you are prepared to go. Your £50 bid is registered by eBay but kept hidden from everybody else. Regardless of your extravagance or impatience, the auction will run to its set closing time.

This is proxy bidding. Baffling, isn't it?

Ready to bid

STATION TO STATION LP (APLI-1327) DAVE BOWIE

Current bid: £15.00

Your maximum bid: £ 25.00 (Enter £16.00 **or more**)

[Place Bid >] You will confirm in the next step.

eBay automatically bids on your behalf **up to** your maximum bid.
Learn about bidding.

When you bid higher than the minimum required, your bid becomes a proxy.

2. Bid late

Like our last-minute bidder in the wardrobe auction, you might prefer to play your cards close to your chest. Come the very end, if the highest bid is still below the maximum that you are prepared to pay, you can throw in a late bid and perhaps seize the auction by stealth. Remember, the auction must close at the set time so it stands to reason that if you bid late enough nobody else will have the time to outbid you.

It's a fine strategy but slightly undermined by the fact that many, many people do just the same. This means that there's every chance you'll be outbid in the closing seconds (or, indeed, very last second). We'll discuss this in some detail later when we look at 'sniping'.

The other snag is that even a high, really late bid can still be beaten by a hidden proxy. Keep reading ...

Starting bid	£4.99
	[Place Bid >]
Time left:	**6 mins 45 secs**
	7-day listing
	Ends 30-Nov-04 08:48:00 GMT
Start time:	23-Nov-04 08:48:00 GMT

Hold your horses until the very end of an auction and you minimise the risk of sparking a bidding frenzy.

3. Pretend it's a live auction

You might decide to play an eBay auction just like a live auction i.e. make a bid, wait to be bettered, bid higher again, wait, bid, wait, bid etc. The seller will doubtless enjoy the action – it's fun watching competition drive up the price of your item, as you will discover when you become an eBay trader yourself – and you may even enjoy the process just as you would in an auction room.

But you won't win. Your opponent(s) may stop bidding and you could easily find yourself sitting as the highest bidder for hours or even days. But it counts for nothing. Think of a runner setting the pace for all 25 laps of a 10,000m final only to be beaten to the line by a sprint finish from the rear.

If there's one universal anecdote about eBay that holds true, it's that all the important action takes place in the closing moments. You could be the highest bidder from start to finish of a ten-day auction and still lose out at the death. In fact, on a popular item, you will almost certainly be beaten by a high last-second bid. Talk about frustrating ...

Bid Amount	Date of bid
£290.00	14-Nov-04 20:38:51 GMT
£280.00	14-Nov-04 20:38:36 GMT
£270.00	14-Nov-04 20:38:17 GMT
£260.00	14-Nov-04 20:38:01 GMT
£245.00	14-Nov-04 20:37:44 GMT
£220.00	14-Nov-04 20:37:26 GMT

Check the bid history on any popular item and you'll likely see a flurry of last-minute bids.

PART  Proxy bidding explored

We'll cover 'proxy bidding' again later (see p96-100) but it's worth considering now for four reasons:

● It's absolutely central to the way eBay works.
● It marks the greatest single difference between eBay and a live auction.
● It's deeply counter-intuitive.
● It's the key to winning auctions.

To understand how proxy bidding operates on eBay, consider this scenario. There's a used Yamaha SG 1000 electric guitar on auction. This is a relatively rare guitar that's sure to attract a lot of interest and could reasonably be expected to fetch £600. We'll suppose that there are three interested parties: Keith, Eric and Dave. Each would happily pay £600 for the guitar, although each would naturally prefer to pay rather less. The auction begins with a starting price of £200 and no reserve (see p121).

Keith, Eric and Dave just can't resist this fine guitar.

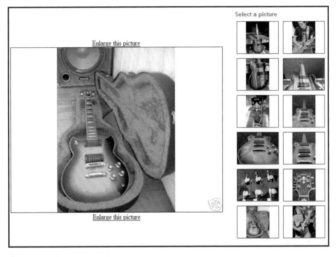

Increment vs proxy

Just as in a live auction controlled by an auctioneer, eBay raises the price by a fixed increment with each new bid. This increment is determined by the current auction price, which is either:

● The minimum starting price (set by the seller), or
● The highest bid placed so far.

For an item with a starting price of £200, the bid increment is £5. See the table opposite for a summary of bid increments.

Keith gets in first with a £200 bid. Eric responds with an incremental bid of £205. He now leads the auction. Keith bids back with £210 and Eric bids again with £215. Dave bides his time.

Now this incremental bidding could continue all the way up to £600 or beyond, as would be the case in a live auction. But it may take a week or more and it would be monumentally tedious for Keith and Eric. However, Keith is a seasoned hand at the eBay game and understands proxy bidding. He understands that he can place a really high bid just once. eBay will then keep his actual

bid value secret but automatically increase his bid by the required increment to ensure that he continues to lead the auction.

eBay determines the bid increment based on the current auction price (these figures are correct at time of writing):

Current price	Bid increment
£0.01–£1.00	£0.05
£1.01–£5.00	£0.20
£5.01–£15.00	£0.50
£15.01–£60.00	£1.00
£60.01–£150.00	£2.00
£150.01–£300.00	£5.00
£300.01–£600.00	£10.00
£600.01–£1,500.00	£20.00
£1,500.01–£3,000.00	£50.00
and up	£100.00

Auction action

In our example, the auction stands at £215 in Eric's favour. Keith now bids a whopping £400. Obviously, he takes the lead. Less obviously, he takes the lead at £220, not £400.

Behind the scenes, eBay is monitoring the auction. It responds to each new bid by bidding on Keith's behalf, but only as high as is necessary to hold the lead. This is always the value of the highest bid plus the minimum bid increment. Here, Eric had bid £215 and the minimum bid increment is £5, so Keith's bid must be £220. Keith now leads the auction.

Eric sees Keith's bid, thinks to himself that he'll go an extra fiver, and bids £225. But alas! The price leaps instantly to £230 with Keith still in the lead. eBay has responded again and upped Keith's bid automatically. Eric bids £235 but the price jumps to £240 in Keith's favour. Keith is sitting at home doing absolutely nothing. Dave still bides his time.

This is proxy bidding at work. Just to be clear:

- Keith has placed a proxy bid of £400. This is the maximum price that he could be required to pay for the guitar.

- However, Keith's actual bid is only ever the highest bid plus the minimum bid increment. That is, when Eric bids £235, the eBay system automatically bids £240 on Keith's behalf – and will continue to do so all the way up to, but not beyond, £400.

- Only when Eric, or somebody else, bids higher than £400 can Keith be beaten.

Ready to bid

STATION TO STATION LP (APLI-1327) DAVE BOWIE

Current bid: £15.00

Your maximum bid: £ 16.00   (Enter £16.00 **or more**)

Place Bid >   You will confirm in the next step.

eBay automatically bids on your behalf **up to** your maximum bid.
Learn about bidding.

Proxy leapfrog

Let's say that Eric tires of placing fiddly incremental bids and being beaten by Keith all the time. He suspects that Keith has placed a high proxy bid because this is the only explanation for why he, Eric, keeps being outbid. But he doesn't know how high Keith is prepared to go. He bids £300 to see what happens. This is still well within his personal maximum. The auction price jumps to £305 in Keith's favour.

Eric now knows for sure that Keith has placed a proxy bid; all that remains is to breach it. He bids £350 and the current price becomes £355. He ups the ante again with a £400 bid but still Keith is in the lead. However, this time the auction price remains at £400. This is because in the event of two or more equal bids, eBay automatically favours the earlier bid. Eric now knows Keith's proxy bid must be £400, for otherwise the price would have jumped to £405. So Eric places his own proxy bid of £450 to comprehensively outbid Keith. He now leads the auction with a bid of £405 i.e. the next highest bid (Keith's £400) plus the minimum bid increment.

Time is ticking by. Dave still bides his time.

Keith now has the dilemma. His earlier proxy bid has been defeated and the auction stands at £405 in Eric's favour. But how high has Eric actually bid? Keith has no way of knowing. The only way to find out is by placing a new bid himself.

If he bids £410, he will either lead the auction or see the price jump to £415 in Eric's favour. The latter would be a sure indication that Eric has placed a proxy bid. Either way, Keith has no chance of winning the guitar unless and until he overtakes Eric.

So he bids £500. This is now the highest bid so the auction price changes to the next highest bid – Eric's £450 – pus the £5 increment. Keith is back in the lead.

And so on and so on. Keith and Eric can play proxy leapfrog until the auction ends at its appointed time. But are they actually achieving anything other than pushing up the value of the guitar?

You Have Been Outbid

ebY.co.uk

Dear ████████,
You are no longer the high bidder on the following eBay item:

YAMAHA SG 1000 (SG1000) ELECTRIC GUITAR - RARE VINTAGE
Re-listed due to scam. Now includes brand new pickguard

Enter stage left ...

With twenty minutes to go in the auction, Dave makes his move. He really wants this guitar and is prepared to pay well. Being a seasoned eBayer, he knows that there will likely be some frantic bidding in the closing minutes so he places a high proxy bid of £606.79. The odd amount is simply a strategy that makes it somewhat harder to guess a hidden proxy value.

This new bid beats all others so eBay adjusts the auction price to the value of the next highest bid – Eric's £500 – plus £5. In other words, Dave takes the lead at £505 backed by a hidden proxy bid of £606.79.

Keith, glued to his browser, watches in dismay. He bids £550 but the auction jumps to £555 with Dave still in the lead. How high is Dave's hidden proxy? He has to beat it to find out. Keith bids his personal maximum of £600 in desperation but the price simply goes to £605.

Time is running out, Keith has already bid his true maximum, and the guitar is slipping from his grasp ...

Desperate measures

Eric, meanwhile, has been watching from the wings with increasing frustration. He sees the auction hit £605 and decides to bid higher. But how much higher? He only has time for one more bid. If he bids £610, he might not overtake Dave's hidden proxy bid and he'll lose. If he bids £700, he might get the guitar for as little £615 (if Dave's proxy was £610) but he might have to pay the full £700 (if Dave's proxy turns out to be £695).

With one minute to go, he compromises and bids £650. This defeats Dave's proxy and Eric takes the lead at £611.79 (remember, the current price is always the highest bid plus the increment: in this case, £606.79 plus £5).

Dave bids back at £625 but it's not enough. The auction jumps to £630 in Eric's favour. Dave doesn't have time to re-bid. He's out of the game.

	Bid	Current Price	Explanation of current price	Current leader	Narrative
Keith	£200.00	£200.00		Keith	Keith opens the bidding
Eric	£205.00	£205.00	(£200 + £5)	Eric	Eric places a winning incremental bid
Keith	£210.00	£210.00	(£205 + £5)	Keith	Keith places a winning incremental bid
Eric	£215.00	£215.00	(£210 + £5)	Eric	Eric places a winning incremental bid
Keith	£400.00	£220.00	(£215 + £5)	Keith	Keith places a winning proxy bid of £400
Eric	£225.00	£230.00	(£225 + £5)	Keith	Eric places an incremental bid but is outbid by Keith's proxy
Eric	£235.00	£240.00	(£235 + £5)	Keith	Eric places an incremental bid but is outbid by Keith's proxy
Eric	£300.00	£305.00	(£300 + £5)	Keith	Eric places a proxy bid but is outbid by Keith's proxy
Eric	£350.00	£355.00	(£350 + £5)	Keith	Eric places a proxy bid but is outbid by Keith's proxy
Eric	£400.00	£400.00	A tie	Keith	Eric places a proxy bid that equals Keith's proxy
Eric	£450.00	£405.00	(£400 + £5)	Eric	Eric places a winning proxy bid
Keith	£500.00	£455.00	(£450 + £5)	Keith	Keith places a winning proxy bid
Dave	£606.79	£505.00	(£500 + £5)	Dave	Dave places a winning proxy bid
Keith	£550.00	£555.00	(£550 + £5)	Dave	Keith places a proxy bid but is outbid by Dave's proxy
Keith	£600.00	£605.00	(£600 + £5)	Dave	Keith places a proxy bid but is outbid by Dave's proxy
Eric	£650.00	£611.79	(£606.79 + £5)	Eric	Eric places a winning proxy bid
Dave	£625.00	£630.00	(£625 + £5)	Eric	Dave places a proxy bid but is outbid by Eric's proxy
Keith	£700.00	£655.00	(£650 + £5)	Keith	Keith places a winning proxy bid
Jimi	£800.00	£705.00	(£700 + £5)	Jimi	Jimi places a winning proxy bid – and wins the auction

With ten seconds left in the auction, Keith convinces himself that he'll never see such a nice guitar on offer at this price again (this is typical auction fever, common to both eBay and live auctions, where dodgy rationalisation eggs us ever onwards). He steels himself and bids £700. eBay looks for the highest bid, which is Eric's £650 proxy, and automatically tops it by the £5 increment. The auction stands at £655 to Keith at only three seconds from victory ...

But along comes Jimi and snipes the auction for £705. If you want to know how he did it – and we strongly suggest that you should – see p101-113.

Risky business

The implications of proxy bidding, both good and bad, should be clear. For one thing, you can place a high proxy bid early on and remain in control of the auction. Nobody knows how high you are prepared to go until they manage to breach your proxy with a higher bid.

If you're the gambling sort, you might choose to bid, say, £1,000 for the guitar. You expect the guitar to reach between £600 and £700, so all you have to do to secure victory is place an unassailable proxy and you'll get it for the price of the highest bid plus the increment.

And, indeed, this strategy can work to your advantage. People may make a few tentative bids but then give up when they realise that there is a high hidden proxy at play. There's nothing more discouraging than making bid after bid but never managing to lead the auction.

But what happens if an equally determined bidder pushes you all the way up to your proxy? You can't simply back out of the auction and withdraw your bid when you see the price going up. In other words, you could conceivably end up paying £995 for an item worth £700 tops – which is a fine way to win a guitar but lose your shirt. :

Here's a summary of the auction action. If you can get your head around proxy bidding, you have what it takes to master eBay.

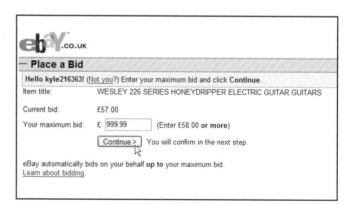

If you really want to win an auction, you can ensure success with a ridiculously high proxy. But on your head be it if somebody else bids you up, up and up.

PART **1**

Live auctions revisited

Compare and contrast proxy bidding with a live auction once again. In a live auction, every bidder shows his or her hand with every bid. True, you never know how high somebody is really prepared to go but getting there is a gradual, incremental, open business of bid beating bid.

In the example discussed earlier, imagine that right at the start somebody had slipped the auctioneer a slip of paper with a 'proxy' bid of £30. The auction begins and you bid £10.

'That's £11 to the gentleman in the corner. Who will bid me £12?'

Puzzled, because you are patently not the gentleman in the corner, you bid £12. 'Now going for £13 to the same gentleman,' says the auctioneer. 'Will anyone bid me £14?'

And so on. Every new bid on your part increases the current auction price but you can never win the wardrobe. Or rather, you can only win the wardrobe by exceeding the proxy bid – and because the proxy bid is hidden, you can only discover what it is by beating it.

That's how eBay works. Little wonder people find it so confusing. Even seasoned traders sometimes struggle to grasp what's going on behind the scenes in a busy auction. However, here are three key things to remember:

● An incremental bid is a bid that exceeds the highest bid by the minimum increment.

● A proxy bid is a bid that exceeds the current auction price by more than the minimum increment. However, the bidder's maximum bid remains hidden until it is exceeded.

● The current auction price is always the second highest bid plus the bid increment.

'GOOD NEWS DARLING! YOU'VE RECEIVED LOADS OF BIDS...'

PART **Summing up**

If the above examples are confusing or even alarming, don't panic. eBay is confusing, at least at first, but you'll soon get the hang of it. Here's a summary of the key similarities and differences:

	Live auction	eBay auction
Who wins?	The highest bidder always wins.	The highest bidder always wins.
When does the auction end?	When nobody is prepared to outbid the current leader.	At a fixed time determined in advance by the seller.
How are bids made?	Each new bid increases the previous bid by a fixed increment, determined by the auctioneer. However, it is always within the bidder's right to shortcut the process by bidding higher than the increment ('£50 for the wardrobe!').	Each new bid increases the previous bid by a fixed increment determined by the current price (see the table on p14). A bidder can choose to bid higher (i.e. place a proxy bid) but the current price reflects only the minimum required to lead the auction.

Forget everything you thought you knew about auctioneering. eBay's proxy bidding changes the ballpark completely.

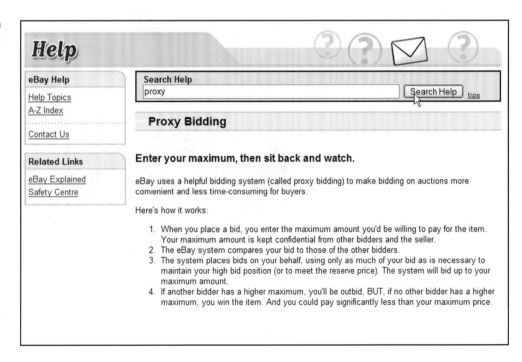

Help

eBay Help

Help Topics
A-Z Index

Contact Us

Related Links

eBay Explained
Safety Centre

Search Help
proxy   [Search Help] tips

Proxy Bidding

Enter your maximum, then sit back and watch.

eBay uses a helpful bidding system (called proxy bidding) to make bidding on auctions more convenient and less time-consuming for buyers.

Here's how it works:

1. When you place a bid, you enter the maximum amount you'd be willing to pay for the item. Your maximum amount is kept confidential from other bidders and the seller.
2. The eBay system compares your bid to those of the other bidders.
3. The system places bids on your behalf, using only as much of your bid as is necessary to maintain your high bid position (or to meet the reserve price). The system will bid up to your maximum amount.
4. If another bidder has a higher maximum, you'll be outbid. BUT, if no other bidder has a higher maximum, you win the item. And you could pay significantly less than your maximum price.

2

eBay MANUAL

PART 2 Introducing eBay

The pros and cons of internet auctions

There are clearly other differences between live auctions and eBay than simply the bidding system and strategies.

Choice and convenience

In a live auction, choice is limited to items listed in the auction on that particular day. Even in a specialist auction where there are many similar items, this increases the impetus to buy. A decent wardrobe may not be a once-in-a-lifetime opportunity but securing a purchase on the day, even at a higher price than you would like, saves you another visit. In contrast, eBay is a global marketplace. Choice is virtually unlimited. Unless you collect Plutonian pebbles, you're sure to find the same items on offer time and time again.

In a live auction, you have to get your goods home. In most cases, goods you buy on eBay will be delivered to your door.

Live auctions certainly have the advantage from a touch-and-feel perspective as you view items in the flesh, as it were, whereas in eBay all you have to go on is the seller's description

Nobody ever accused eBay of being short on choice.

(and photographs) of an item. However, it is in every regular trader's interest to be scrupulously accurate about what is for sale. You can usually rely on descriptions and clarify issues by asking the seller a pertinent question.

As a seller, too, you reach a far greater market with eBay than you could in a lifetime of visiting auction rooms.

Competition

In an auction room, a bidder is up against whoever else is in the room (or occasionally on the end of a telephone line), but that's it. In an eBay auction, you are competing with the world. What's more, it's a world that's increasingly savvy with the ins and outs of internet auctioneering. Two years ago, you could win any online auction with the right price; today, you have to take on sharp operators at their own game. This book will teach you how.

As a seller, you'll find a vast and willing market but you'll also find the competition tough. If something can conceivably be marketed on eBay, it will be. Your chance of being the first to come up with a novel money-spinning idea is slim but they do, at least, exist. In many areas, though, there's plenty of room for everyone (see Appendix 2 for an example).

Tactics and pressure

Live auctions are daunting, personal affairs. Real people compete with each other in a real room and you may almost find it rude to outbid that dear old granny with her eye on a teapot. In eBay, auctions are virtual. Personalities and eye contact just don't come into it. The computer screen is a barrier between you and reality but it's a permeable barrier that you can use to your advantage. Auctions go on for days rather than minutes so there's less pressure to think quickly and less necessity to bid impulsively.

You only really have one tactic in a live auction: bid higher than anybody else. True, coming in late gives you an element of surprise, and bidding quickly, confidently or aggressively can rattle other bidders, but ultimately it's just a question of being prepared to pay the most. In eBay, tactics are critical, as we shall discuss at length. For now, let's just note that winning an eBay auction is a threefold matter:

● You must make the highest bid ...
● But you must make it in the right way ...
● And you must make it at the right time.

Legalities and fraud

Thoughts about the potential for fraud and rip-offs on eBay may be running rampant in your mind right now, and we suggest that this is no bad thing. It is extremely important to appreciate that you use eBay almost entirely at your own risk. Yes, a winning bidder and seller are legally obliged to see the contract through to completion but remember the nature of the medium: eBay operates on the internet, not in an auction room, and there is no auctioneer to see things through on your behalf. You don't really know who you're dealing with when you engage in an online auction; and, unless the other party is prepared to offer some form of positive verification, you can't really find out. A seller may register with a fake ID and stolen credit card, take your money and fail to ship the goods. Despite some good intentions, eBay is pretty powerless to do anything about it.

That's the bottom line. Buyer – and, to a lesser extent, seller – beware.

However, there are also some good reasons why, by and large, eBay 'just works'.

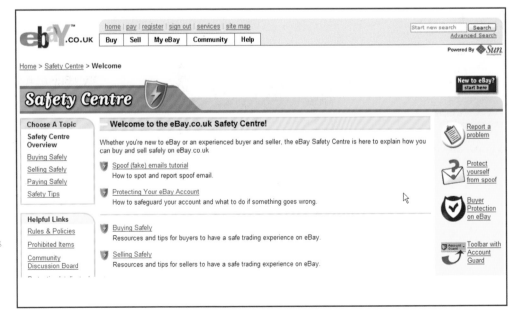

eBay does its bit to protect traders – check out the Safety Centre for sound advice – but buying and selling online is not without its risks.

INTRODUCING eBay

The eBay community

The sweet and surprising but equally rather alarming fact is that eBay has always run on the principle and practice of trust. A seller who describes an item perfectly, even in a slightly deprecatory fashion, will be rewarded with glowing feedback when a buyer discovers the item to be as good or better than expected. A seller who over-sells an item, ignoring flaws or conveniently forgetting to point out important factors, will be quietly but effectively reprimanded with neutral feedback. A downright crook will be slated with negative feedback and shouldn't be around too long. Buyers and sellers are expected to work through their own difficulties and, by and large, they do just that.

However, what of all the millions of newcomers to the eBay marketplace? Many, we suspect, fail to see the significance of feedback (see p45) and rush in blindly in pursuit of a bargain. Many, we fear, let enthusiasm distort reality and try to make a quick buck by selling outright tat (there's a market for tat, as for everything, but describing it as something other is dishonest). Many more people are undoubtedly just inexperienced in the ways of the internet and online shopping in general, let alone the complexities of eBay. Such people are vulnerable to the scam merchants that eBay inevitably attracts.

The key is understanding how eBay works and then making it work for you. That's why we wrote this book.

With well over 100 million registered users, the eBay community is well able to help its own.

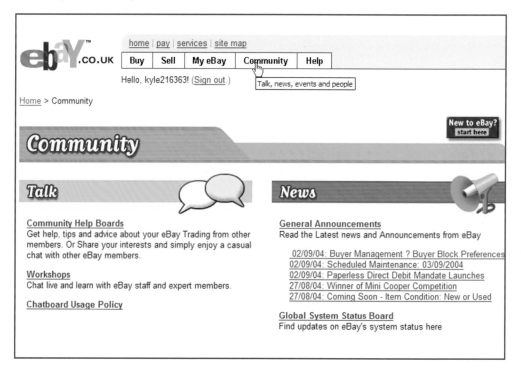

Self-support system

The vast majority of people who trade on eBay for fun or for business are honest and helpful. Many have grown with the service as it has evolved, and they appreciate that on eBay a reputation is everything. Ask a seller a question and you'll doubtless receive a full answer whether or not you have placed a bid. If you have a problem completing a purchase, chances are you'll find a sympathetic ear eager to work things out.

We're sure that many old-time eBayers miss the old days when the site was more like a club than a global phenomenon; when participants measured in hundreds of thousands rather than tens of millions; and when you could set up a specialist shop without immediately seeing your idea copied by all and sundry. However, many smart traders are predisposed to help the 'newbie' and help is never far away.

Unfortunately, eBay's own Help system is (how can we put this tactfully?) positively Byzantine. It's a useful first base, sometimes, but we strongly recommend that you also scout around the super-friendly user forums (called Help Boards) when you have a problem or a query. If the concept of proxy bidding makes your brain hurt, thrash out the issues to your own satisfaction in a discussion forum before committing real money in a real auction.

See **http://pages.eBay.co.uk/community/chat/index.html**.

Try the 'New to eBay' Help Board for a good introduction to the workings of eBay.

Welcome to the 'New to eBay' Board!
hnutford@ebay.com (view author's auctions)
01/09/04 12:16 (Report)

Hullo there,

Welcome to eBay! eBay is the world's largest online marketplace. Every day millions of people come together to buy and sell.

But we know that using eBay isn't always easy, especially when you are new. eBay has it's own rules and foibles that you'll learn along the. And as you get started it can be useful to have a friendly bunch of people to help you along.

That's why we have created this board. It's a specific forum for newbies on eBay.

If you have a question to ask, the best option is to start your own discussion. That way more people will see your question and offer answers. To start a discussion thread of your own, log into the board with your eBay ID and click "Add Discussion" at the bottom of the page.

You may find these Help resources useful as you start out:

The Help Centre: http://pages.ebay.co.uk/help/index.html

eBay Explained: http://pages.ebay.co.uk/ebayexplained/

Services Hub: http://pages.ebay.co.uk/services/index.html

Tours: http://pages.ebay.co.uk/education/tours.html

PART  The eBay User Agreement

Pretty much anybody can use eBay UK but by doing so you bind yourself to a comprehensive User Agreement. You should, of course, read this in full – follow the User Agreement link at the foot of the eBay home page, **www.ebay.co.uk** – but here are some salient points:

- You have to be 18 or older.
- You'll need an internet connection and a computer.
- You must have a valid email address.
- You may need a credit card (see p29).
- You must not let anybody else use your eBay account, so keep your password secret.
- 'eBay is Only a Venue'. Note the emphatic capitalisation. The nub here is that eBay provides the means for buyers and sellers to meet one another and trade. It does not assume the role of auctioneer and your rights of redress are thus limited. In particular, eBay is 'not responsible for ensuring that buyers and sellers actually complete a transaction'.
- You are, however, legally bound to pay for any item which you win at auction, providing the terms of the sale are lawful. And if you are the seller, you are bound to complete the transaction except in extraordinary circumstances, such as the winning bidder refusing to make payment.
- You can't bid on your own items or get friends to artificially boost the price ('shill' bidding). That's considered cheating and can have you thrown out of eBay. Rightly so.
- Sellers must pay eBay all appropriate fees. This bit is rather important as eBay makes money from sellers. From a buyer's perspective, you can register with eBay, bid on auctions, win items and make payments without ever owing eBay a penny. But when you want to sell, you become subject to an intricate (and ever-changing) fee structure (see p122-123 for details).

Daunting it may be but it's important to read and understand the User Agreement.

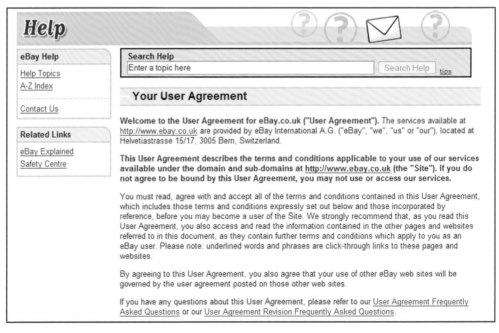

PART 2 What can and can't I sell?

Do you have a fantastic idea for a great product to sell on eBay? The first rule is that you must operate lawfully. This means selling only items that are themselves legal and that you are legally entitled to sell. You cannot, for instance, sell firearms, drugs or stolen goods. You can only sell computer software if you abide by the terms of the licence and copyright – you can't simply burn your copy of Windows onto recordable CDs and sell it 100 times over – and you can't sell body parts (even your own, up to and including your soul).

Football tickets can only be sold by registered dealers and with the prior consent of eBay; and airplane and train tickets are barred.

The full list of prohibited and 'questionable' items can be found here: **http://pages.ebay.co.uk/help/community/png-items.html**.

However, in the real world of frenetic online trading, none of this means very much. With judicious searching and a little reading between the lines, you can find many supposedly banned items with little effort. eBay certainly does not condone such trading but its policing policy verges on the toothless: offending auctions may be cancelled and 'disciplinary action may range from a formal warning, up to indefinite suspension of a member's account'.

Regardless, as a buyer or a seller you are well advised to stay within the law. If you wish to report an item for sale that you believe may contravene eBay's terms or be illegal, use the form here:

http://pages.ebay.co.uk/help/contact_inline/index.html

eBay restricts the sale of certain goods and services.

Is my item allowed on eBay UK?
Prohibited, Questionable & Infringing Items

eBay is here to help, but you are ultimately responsible for making sure that buying an item or selling your item(s) is allowed on eBay and is not prohibited in the eyes of the law. Follow these steps to find out whether or not your item can be listed on eBay.

- First, review eBay's listing policies. These guidelines will help you properly list items and understand what is allowed on eBay.
- If you're still unsure about listing your particular item, look over the select list of items below. These guidelines and policies are designed to help you trade safely on eBay. Remember that:

1. **"Prohibited"**
   means that these items may **not** be listed on eBay.
2. **"Questionable"**
   means that items may be listed under certain conditions.
3. **"Potentially Infringing"**
   means that items may be in violation of certain copyrights, trademarks or other rights. For your protection, some items here are not allowed ("prohibited"), regardless of the legality of these particular items, because they almost always violate copyright or trademark laws.

	Questionable
Aeroplane Tickets	Adults Only
Alcohol	Artefacts
Animals and Wildlife Products	Autographed Items
Catalogue and URL Sales	Batteries
Counterfeit Currency and Stamps	British Titles
Counterfeit and Trademarked Items	CFC and HCFC Refrigerants
Credit Cards	Contracts and Tickets
Drugs and Drug paraphernalia	Electronics Equipment
Embargoed Items & Prohibited Countries	

PART 2 Signing up

You can browse eBay without restrictions but if you want to place a bid, you'll need an eBay account. Registration is free and pretty straightforward so we'll just skip through the main steps here.

*Open your browser at **www.ebay.co.uk** and click Register. Note that you can only register with your local version of eBay so if you live in the UK that means eBay UK. However, once you're in the club, so to speak, you can bid on items hosted by any of the regional versions, such as **ebay.com** (US), **ebay.fr** (France) and **ebay.com.au** (Australia).*

With well over 114 million registered members and rising, you may well struggle to find a unique ID or user name. If your preferred choice is already in use, you'll have the chance to choose an alternative later. We suggest that you do not use your real name, as your trading history will be publicly accessible on eBay and you may not wish to be personally identified. Be sure to create a secure password that would be impossible to guess.

Should you lose your password, eBay will send it to you at the email address specified during registration. However, you'll have to answer a secret question first to prove you are who you say you are. The answer to the question you select need not be true, but it should be memorable.

4

Here I have just been told that my chosen User ID is already in use. Note that IDs are always expressed in lower case so my use of capitals in Step 2 was pointless. Oh well, live and learn. You may have to try a few possibilities before you hit upon something that nobody else has thought of. Don't worry too much about your ID, though: you'll end up selling to and buying from some very odd-sounding eBay traders as time goes by. See also p161 for a cautionary word on picking a name that identifies you.

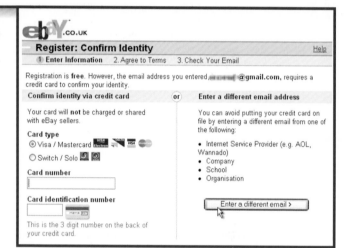

eBay Registration: Enter Information

① Enter Information   2 Agree to Terms   3 Check Your Email

⚠ The User ID **kylemacrae** you requested has already been taken. Please try one of the two options below.

Let eBay suggest some User IDs   or   Create another eBay User ID

Name up to 3 of your favourite things: eBay User ID

[   ] [   ] [   ]   [kyle216363]

5

Now here's a curious thing. If you try to sign up with an 'anonymous' web-based email service such as Hotmail, Yahoo or, in my case, Gmail, eBay forces you to register a credit card at this point. Although this is purely to verify your identity, you may be uncomfortable about being asked to produce such details. If so, select an alternative email address if you can. The one provided by your ISP is fine here (yourname@wanadoo.com, for instance). If you have your own domain name – www.anythingatall.co.uk – use it instead.

eb Y.CO.UK

Register: Confirm Identity   Help

① Enter Information   2. Agree to Terms   3. Check Your Email

Registration is **free**. However, the email address you entered, ~~~~~@gmail.com, requires a credit card to confirm your identity.

Confirm identity via credit card   or   **Enter a different email address**

Your card will **not** be charged or shared with eBay sellers.

You can avoid putting your credit card on file by entering a different email from one of the following:

Card type
◉ Visa / Mastercard
○ Switch / Solo

• Internet Service Provider (e.g. AOL, Wannadoo)
• Company
• School
• Organisation

Card number
[   ]

[Enter a different email >]

Card identification number
[   ]

This is the 3 digit number on the back of your credit card.

6

When your alternative email address is accepted, or if you register your credit card, you'll find yourself at the User Agreement. Read this (there's a summary on p26) and click Accept. That's it: you're now an eBay member … almost.

I accept the eBay User Agreement and the terms and conditions incorporated by reference. I have read the Privacy Policy and I specifically acknowledge and accept the following:

☑ **I must be an adult (18 years old) to trade on eBay and I certify that I am an adult and can enter into this Agreement.**

☑ I agree to be contacted by eBay in accordance with the default settings of my **Notification Preferences** and understand that I can change those preferences at any time by going to the Notification Preferences page in my eBay.

[I Accept >]

7

First, log into your email account and look for an automatic confirmation message. Click the link contained within it to activate your account. Until you do this, you'll be unable to log in to the eBay website as a member. In other words, if you entered a fake email address in Step 5, retrace your steps and try again!

Please note that this is a system generated email. Please do not reply to this email. If you have questions, please click the following link or paste it in your browser. http://pages.ebay.co.uk/help/basics/select-support.html

eb Y.CO.UK

To complete eBay registration, you must click the button below.

[Complete eBay Registration >]

If the button above does not work:

1. Write down this confirmation code: 13060
2. Type in or copy and paste this link into your Web browser: http://pages.ebay.co.uk/register
   Make sure you copy this link exactly and do not add extra spaces.
3. Enter your confirmation code.

If you need additional help, contact eBay's Customer Support.

PART

Finding your way around

The first thing to do, we suggest, is log in to eBay, check
your account details and get a feel for the place. Point
your browser at **www.ebay.co.uk** and bookmark the page
for future reference. You'll return here whenever you want
to log in for a new session.

*Click the Sign In link at the very top of the screen. On
the page shown here, enter your User ID and password.
The 'keep me signed in' option is theoretically useful,
but eBay periodically asks you for your password
regardless of this setting. If there's any actual pattern
governing when you need to re-enter your password
and when you don't, we cannot fathom it.*
Once inside, you can use the Browse, Search or Sell

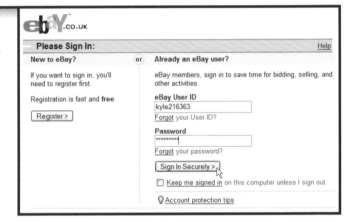

*buttons at the top of the page to explore current
auctions or list an item of your own (a Buy button
sometimes replaces Browse and Search). These will be
your launch pads of the future. But first click the My
eBay button or link to open your personal page.*

*Your User ID is displayed here along with your
Feedback rating in brackets. Having not yet traded on
eBay, you currently rank a big fat zero. Further down
the page, look for the My Account link in the left-hand
sidebar and click Personal Information.*

4

On this page, you can check and, if necessary, amend the details you fed the system during registration. You might want to use your business rather than your home address for deliveries because somebody will always be there; if so, click the Addresses link and add your business (or any alternative) address.

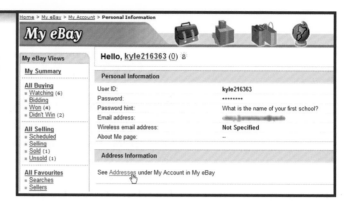

5

Click the Community button at the top of the page to access eBay announcements and user forums (Community Help Boards). The former are always worth a read and the latter can prove tremendously helpful if you need advice from your peers. Whatever your question, chances are that somebody has asked and had it answered recently.

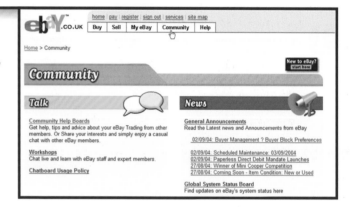

6

Here, for instance, is a discussion on the 'New to eBay' Help Board. This demonstrates the spirit of the eBay community: you can get unlimited, free and practical (although unofficial) advice from fellow traders who have learned their own lessons the hard way and are prepared to help newcomers untangle eBay's knottier areas.

My buyer wants their money back?

(118 ⭐) (view author's auctions)
05/10/04 19:47 (Report)

I sold my car about 4 weeks ago through ebay. I was very honest, and sold the car with a MOT. The week previous to selling the car I took it to my local garage and they replaced the brake pads.
Well to cut a long story short, the person who bought the car rang me this morning and said her garage said the car is undriveable and that she wants her money back.
If I had thought the car was undriveable I would not have sold it. As I said the car was MOT'ed, and had just had a full service from the main dealer, plus the brake pads from the week before.
Any thoughts? What are my rights if she wanted to take this further?

_____

(0) me (view author's auctions)
05/10/04 19:59(#1 of 2) (Report)

Selling a secondhand car on ebay should be no different to selling one anywhere. You don't offer any guarantees, as long as it was as you described it the buyer is not eligible for a refund. Besides, if it had an MOT and a recent full service it can hardly be undriveable.

7

Finally for now, click the Help link. You'll find it at the top of every eBay page. This is a searchable index where you can enter key words or phrases (e.g. 'forgotten password') to get answers. Try the A–Z Index as well. If you find that the eBay Help system leaves you more confused than you were before, return to the Help Boards.

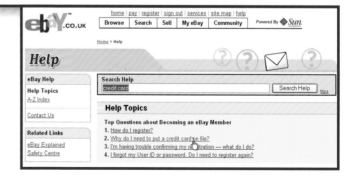

PART 2 Searching eBay

eBay UK is vast and growing every day. This is good news for prospective shoppers as it means more choice, but sometimes the sheer choice is overwhelming. How on earth do you stand a chance of finding something that you want to bid for and buy?

Here's how.

1

Back on the eBay home page, log in and click Buy or Browse. Browsing is a way of looking for auction items by category. Let's say you want to buy a wardrobe (having lost out in the live auction earlier). Click the 'See all categories' link at the bottom of the page to expand the full category index.

Consumer Electronics
Audio - Separates & Systems | TV & Home Cinema...

Crafts

Dolls & Bears
Dolls | Bears...

DVD, Film & TV
DVDs | Videos: VHS/ PAL (UK)...

Home & Garden
Decorative Items | Garden | DIY...

Health & Beauty

Jewellery & Watches
Watches | Contemporary Fine Jewellery...

Tickets & Travel
Tickets | Travel...

Toys & Games
Diecast & Vehicles | Action Figures & Accessories...

Wholesale & Job Lots...

Everything Else...

See all categories...
See all previous categories...

2

Some guesswork is required here. One of the top-level categories, Home & Garden, seems a likely choice but there's not room on the page to display all the sub-categories. Click the See all link to expand the list further.

See all Automotive categories...

Books, Comics & Magazines (218081)
Antiquarian Books (Pre-1940) (7876)
Audio Books (6300)
Children's Books (23033)
Educational/ Textbooks (13731)
Fiction Books (49479)
First Editions (7430)
Non-Fiction Books (69865)
Comics (21002)
Magazines (19365)

See all Books, Comics & Magazines categories...

Business, Office & Industrial

Dining Room (1655)
DIY (6920)
Food & Drink (2448)
Garden (10760)
Household Appliances (3619)
Kitchen (7606)
Lighting (2976)
Living Room (4544)
Pet Food & Accessories (7508)
Rugs (882)
Other Home, Garden & Family (3483)

See all Home, Garden & Family categories...

Jewellery & Watches (96302)
Beads (6171)

Golf (11605)
Hiking (2031)
Hunting (2885)
Ice Skating (287)
Inline & Roller Skating (4
Kitesurfing (110)
Martial Arts (1724)
Paintball (437)
Rock Climbing (454)
Rugby (963)
Running (880)
Scooters (676)
SCUBA & Snorkelling (2'
Skateboarding (1391)
Skiing (1558)
Snowboarding (926)
Snooker & Pool (1005)

3

You now see a truly impressive list of possibilities. Try using your browser's search function to find words on this very busy page. In Internet Explorer, click Edit, then Find On This Page, enter your keyword and click Find Next. Sure enough, here's a Wardrobe and Storage entry in the Bedroom sub-category. The bracketed figure tells us that there are 861 likely items. Click the link.

Cabinets & Shelving (109)
Plumbing (192)
Towels & Mats (619)
Other Bathroom (234)

Bedroom (6339)
Beds & Mattresses (1265)
Bed Linen & Bedspreads (2668)
Pillows, Duvets & Blankets (917)
Wardrobes & Storage (861)
Other Bedroom (628)

Cleaning, Laundry & Storage (1044)
Cleaning Products & Supplies (282)
Ironing Boards & Laundry Bins (101)
Storage (308)
Other Cleaning & Laundry (353)

④

Some important display options here. At the top of the Search Options column is a choice between items being sold in the UK or, for a broader choice, worldwide. Bear in mind that while buying a DVD from the US may make sense, you'll struggle to find a trader prepared to ship a wardrobe across the Atlantic. Plus you'll have to pay the postage ...

⑤

By default, items are listed by auction closing time, with those auctions ending soonest at the top. Use the drop-down box to rearrange the list in a number of ways. Remember, though, that most of the bidding action typically takes place near the end of an auction so you should be able to get a good idea of the current market rate for the kind of wardrobe you're interested in.

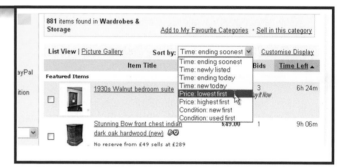

⑥

Get a feel for the level of interest in wardrobes by noting how many bids have been made on items. Here we see a 'Lebus Walnut Wardrobe' going for £16 with 6 hours left on the clock. 16 bidders have been involved in the auction so far – compared to none at all for the item immediately above it – so this looks like a relatively popular item.

⑦

We have one problem here, which is that a great number of items listed here are not wardrobes at all but other forms of bedroom storage (and non-bedroom storage too, for that matter). To narrow the listings down, use the search utility. Enter keyword **wardrobe** in the search field and leave Wardrobes & Storage selected in the adjacent field. Click the Search button. eBay will return only items from within the Wardrobes & Storage category that match. We now have a smaller list of 228 items.

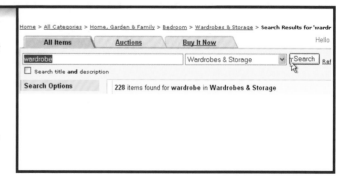

Note the little option below the search field: Search title and description. A default search will only find items that have the word 'wardrobe' in the auction title, whereas somebody selling a bunch of bedroom furniture might only mention the wardrobe in the fuller description. By running the search again with this option checked, we uncover 300 hits.

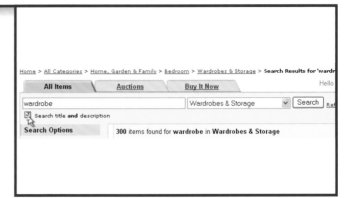

The big trouble with using eBay's category-based Browse feature is that you will only ever find items that have been listed in the correct or appropriate category. For instance, using the method just discussed, you might never find a perfectly suitable wardrobe listed in the Cleaning, Laundry & Storage category (like this one). We say 'might' because it's possible for items to be listed in more than one category. *See p122 for more on this.*

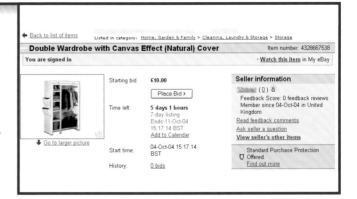

An alternative and usually more profitable method of finding eBay items is via the built-in search engine. On the home page, enter your key word(s) and click Search. The system will return all matching items regardless of category. Again, you have an option to limit your search to items located in the UK or further afield.

Alternatively, use the Advanced link to open a full search page with plenty of useful options. You can exclude specific words or terms, specify the condition, restrict your search to specific categories and determine how the listings appear on the page. A few moments spent here can save you time fine-tuning results later.

Enter keywords here. You can search the entire eBay database or restrict your search to specific categories.

Check this box to search item descriptions as well as titles.

By default, eBay finds auctions that match all of your keywords. Here, you can instruct it to find auctions that match any keyword.

Minimum and maximum prices reflect the current selling price in a live auction. The closer the auction is to closing, the higher the price will be (usually).

Only of interest if you're looking for multiple identical items.

Limit your search to Buy It Now auctions and/or auctions that accept PayPal and/or auctions for new items only.

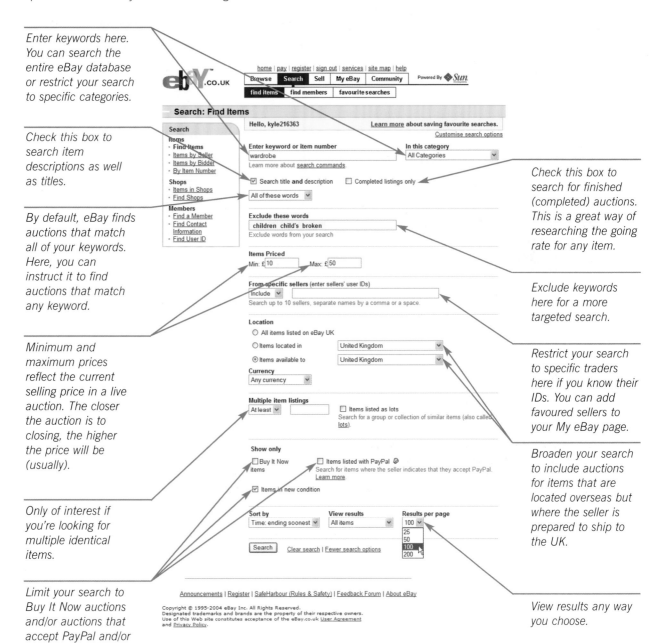

Check this box to search for finished (completed) auctions. This is a great way of researching the going rate for any item.

Exclude keywords here for a more targeted search.

Restrict your search to specific traders here if you know their IDs. You can add favoured sellers to your My eBay page.

Broaden your search to include auctions for items that are located overseas but where the seller is prepared to ship to the UK.

View results any way you choose.

As a rule, don't use the Search titles and descriptions option unless you simultaneously restrict your search to specific categories in the Advanced Search page. Without this restriction, you'll find every item on eBay that contains even a passing reference to wardrobe ('an essential wardrobe accessory' etc.). In our example, we had 951 hits when we conducted an all-category/titles and descriptions search for wardrobe even when we specified a top (current) price of £50, new condition and excluded children's furniture (see Step 11). Words that you exclude in an advanced search are prefixed with a minus sign.

The same search on item titles only returned a mere 25 items, some of which were right on the nose. However, we kept coming across listings for books and paraphernalia related to The Lion, The Witch and The Wardrobe. This is easily remedied by excluding the key words 'lion' and 'witch' in the advanced search page (Step 11). Alternatively, you can prefix words you want to exclude with a minus sign directly in the search field. Hit the Search button again for a refined selection.

In this example, we now have a mere 15 hits matching a wardrobe in new condition available to the UK and currently priced at between £10 and £50, with no lions or witches in sight. There are still a couple of erroneous entries in our hits, including a 'DISNEY TINKERBELL Petite Princess Wardrobe Toy Set', but plenty of items that fit the bill perfectly.

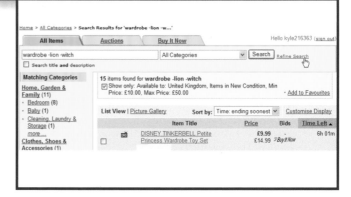

Searching and browsing are by no means exclusive. When you search for a keyword, note the Matching Categories column on the left. This gives you a good idea of which categories harbour most hits. In our wardrobe example, the Bedroom sub-category of Home & Garden is obviously fruitful territory. Remember, these 8 results match our pricing, condition and key word exclusion criteria. At any time, you can click the Refine Search link to reopen the Advanced Search page and make further tweaks.

Understanding 'hits'

When you conduct any (well, almost any) search on eBay, you'll be rewarded with a page or more of hits. Often, you'll have dozens of pages to explore. These pages are busy, so here's a note of what to look for.

The standard simple search field. Remember to check the titles and descriptions box if your need to expand your search.

Check one of these tabs to show only those items that do not have Buy It Now price (Auctions) or only those that do (Buy It Now).

Click here to see only auctions adorned with thumbnail pictures. An unnecessarily restrictive option, in our opinion.

Use this drop-down menu to re-sort auctions by time, price, condition (i.e. new or not new) or whether or not PayPal is accepted.

This sidebar shows how hits are spread throughout eBay categories. Click any link to see only hits within that category.

A thumbnail picture of the auction item.

Redefine the terms of your search here. For intance, expand the search to items located worldwide or narrow it to those that include a Buy It Now price (see p92).

Auction title. Click any blue underlined link to go to the auction page for that item.

The green camera icon means that there are pictures of the item 'inside' despite the lack of a thumbnail.

The current price (which may be backed by a higher, hidden proxy bid) and the number of bids to date.

Click any column header – Price, PayPal, Time Left – to re-sort the entire list of hits by that criteria. For instance, to see the cheapest items at the top, click Price, to reverse order and see the most expensive items first, click Price again.

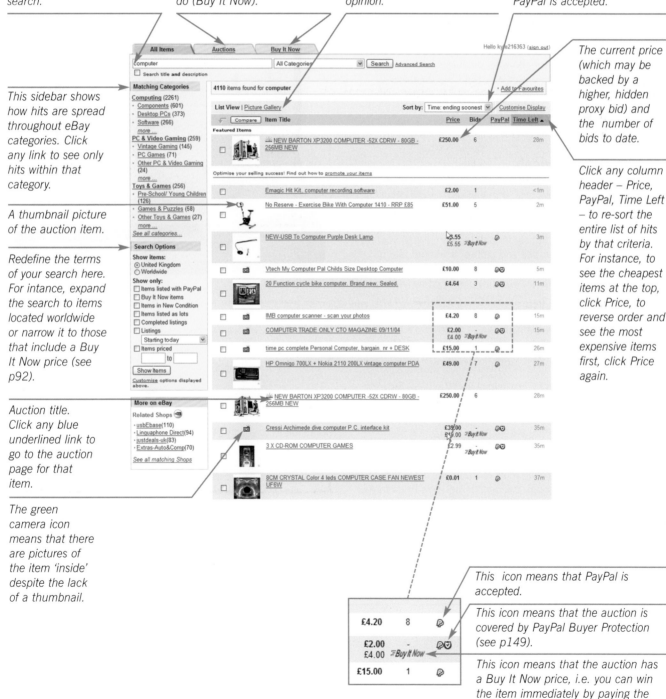

This icon means that PayPal is accepted.

This icon means that the auction is covered by PayPal Buyer Protection (see p149).

This icon means that the auction has a Buy It Now price, i.e. you can win the item immediately by paying the asking price.

Advanced searching

We've looked already at browsing eBay categories and using the search box but there are several ways in which to improve your results and find items more quickly. That's the name of the game, after all: every minute wasted on unsuitable listings means a minute less to snap up a bargain. You could even miss the end of an auction if it takes an age to retrieve the right item from a hundred pages of hits. Worse, you might never find the item at all. eBay is a vast and ever-changing database, and its scale alone is both a virtue and a problem. But it's a database compiled by people, not machines, and thus is riddled with inaccuracies, mistakes and quirks. The trick is giving yourself the best possible chance of finding just the right item in the shortest time and with the least possible hassle.

Use keywords wisely

In Step 13 on p36, we used a minus sign to exclude certain words from a search. Let's look at this in some more detail.

When you enter more than one word into eBay's search box, the system retrieves only item listings in which all of the words appear. For instance, searching for **dell laptop** returns only listings that mention both **dell** and **laptop**. It will not return listings for laptops where the brand Dell doesn't get a mention; nor for Dell items that are not explicitly described as laptops. More on that in a moment. Note that eBay searches are not case-sensitive.

On the other hand, you may get plenty of irrelevant hits that include descriptions like this:

'This laptop is similar to Dell model XYZ ...'

'Better than a Dell!'

'See our other auctions for computers from Dell, HP, Tiny etc ...'

Indeed, canny traders will deliberately include alternative or similar brand names in their item descriptions precisely so that you'll see their listings when searching for something else. Who knows – you might decide to bid on a non-Dell laptop should you stumble upon something equally attractive by chance.

The easiest way to filter out most of these hits is by leaving the Search titles and descriptions box unchecked. This restricts your search to auction titles alone, which filters out much of the junk that traders throw into expanded descriptions.

But what if the item is described as a Dell notebook? Notebook is, after all, an alternative but common name for a laptop. If you do as we just suggested and search for **dell laptop** in item titles, you'll miss all Dell notebooks.

Computers and related hardware and software are big business on eBay. So big, in fact, that finding the right item takes careful searching.

Your instinct might be to include both keywords **laptop** and **notebook** in your search, for that would find both. Or would it? But remember, an eBay search returns only items where all search terms are included. If you search for **dell notebook laptop**, you'll miss all **dell notebook** items and all **dell laptop** items and only find auctions in which the words **dell**, **notebook** and **laptop** all appear. What's more, unless you broaden your search to include item descriptions (which means many more irrelevant hits), you'll only find items where the three keywords appear in the auction title itself.

There's no magic answer here, but you can and should take further steps to increase the accuracy of your searching.

A simple search like this will find you a Dell laptop or two (or 200) but also much else besides.

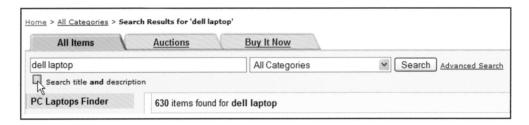

Use multiple keywords

Be as precise as possible, but always be conscious of the fact that precision narrows down searches. This can work for better or for worse.

For instance, if you're looking for a precise model of laptop, include the model in the search. Let's say you want a Dell Inspiron 5100. Here are some possible searches along with their results:

Search terms	Search in:	Hits
dell laptop	Titles and descriptions	1962
dell laptop	Title only	439
dell laptop inspiron	Titles and descriptions	381
dell laptop inspiron	Title only	92
dell laptop inspiron 5100	Titles and descriptions	47
dell laptop inspiron 5100	Title only	5

By throwing in a general model (**inspiron**) and then a precise model number (**5100**) and by variously including and excluding auction descriptions, we narrowed hits from nearly 2,000 to 5.

Let's try that same search now with the term 'notebook' in place of 'laptop'.

Search terms	Search in:	Hits
dell notebook	Titles and descriptions	639
dell notebook	Title only	61
dell notebook inspiron	Titles and descriptions	257
dell notebook inspiron	Title only	10
dell notebook inspiron 5100	Titles and descriptions	38
dell notebook inspiron 5100	Title only	2

Incidentally, the two hits from the **dell notebook inspiron 5100** *titles-only* search appeared among the five hits in our **dell laptop inspiron 5100** *titles-only* search. Why? Because the trader very wisely used this as his auction title: 'DELL INSPIRON 5100 LAPTOP NOTEBOOK'. By including both search terms in the auction title, he made certain the items would be returned in any and all of the above searches. It may make ungainly reading but it's a perfect object lesson in how to make the most of keywords.

The above results seem to indicate that the term 'laptop' is still more commonly used than 'notebook'. However, you would have to run two separate searches to be sure of finding the right laptop/notebook. Unless …

A mere two hits but both of them spot on.

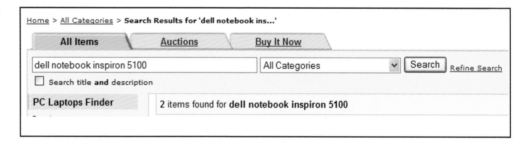

Use either/or expressions

In eBay, you can specify that two or more terms should function as either/or alternatives in a single search. In other words, you can ask for listings for Dell laptops or Dell notebooks. This ensures that you won't miss a potentially good item and saves you the bother of having to repeat a search.

The syntax for an either/or search is simple: enclose your keywords in brackets with a comma but no space between them. For instance, **dell (notebook,laptop)** returns any item that includes the term 'dell' plus *either* 'notebook' *or* 'laptop' *or* (but not necessarily this time) both. By way of comparison, we repeated the search above with this syntax in place:

Search terms	Search in:	Hits
dell (laptop,notebook)	Titles and descriptions	2183
dell (laptop,notebook)	Title only	455
dell (laptop,notebook) inspiron	Titles and descriptions	486
dell (laptop,notebook) inspiron	Title only	92
dell (laptop,notebook) inspiron 5100	Titles and descriptions	51
dell (laptop,notebook) inspiron 5100	Title only	6

These are pretty appealing results. If you know that you definitely want a Dell Inspiron, you have 92 extremely promising hits to browse, or 486 if you figure that the seller may have forgotten to include the model name in the auction title. If you definitely want the 5100 model, you have six sure-fire results.

Either/or expressions are essential when you need to cast a wide search net.

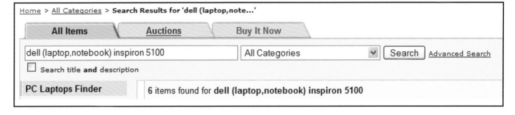

Throw in a wild card

What if you're looking for a Dell Inspiron 5-series laptop but not necessarily the 5100 model? One option is obvious: leave '5100' out of your search terms. However, this will doubtless throw up listings for Inspiron 3000, 4000, 7000 and 8000 series laptops. The way around is this to include a wild card character in the relevant search term. This is simply an asterisk that tells the search engine to look for words that begin with the part of the word before the symbol but have any possible ending. For instance, **Dell (laptop,notebook) inspiron 51*** returns hits that include 51, 5100 and 5150.

It's not a faultless strategy, however. In our example, we had a

Use an asterisk to leave word endings open-ended.

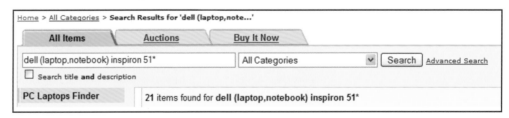

hit with 'Dell Inspiron 8200 laptop with 512MB of RAM'. However, it's a fine way of increasing the range of possibilities, and particularly useful if you need to include possible plurals or alternative word conjugations. For instance, **stamp*** will return 'stamp', 'stamps', 'stamped' and 'stampede'.

You can also use wild cards in the middle of words. **St*mp** will give you 'stamp', 'stump' and 'stomp'. The one restriction is that you must have two or more letters or numbers in your search term before the wild card symbol. While **d*ll** should theoretically give you 'dell', 'dull' and 'doll', eBay won't allow the search.

Use phrases

Another technique which may be familiar to you if you use search engines on the web is the use of quotation marks to define and delineate phrases. For instance, a search for **"dell laptop"** returns only items in which the words 'dell' and 'laptop' appear together as a phrase. Items described as 'laptop from Dell', 'Dell's best laptop' and 'Dell Lap Top' (all real examples, and all potentially of interest) would be excluded. On the other hand, 'This laptop is better than a Dell' and 'Dell desktop system: see my other auctions for a selection of laptops' would also be excluded.

Quotation marks are particularly useful for names and titles. For instance, use **"james last"** rather than **james last** to find recordings by James Last while excluding 'Last chance to buy James Thurber's latest best seller at this price!!'.

However, be careful not to be too specific. If you search for **"the rise and fall of ziggy stardust and the spiders from mars"**, you will probably find some copies of David Bowie's classic album. But you'll also miss all manner of possibilities, including:

'The Rise & Fall Of Ziggy Stardust & The Spiders From Mars'
'The Rise And Fall Of Ziggy Stardust'
'Ziggy Stardust And The Spiders From Mars'

Better by far, we suggest, to include **"ziggy stardust"** as a phrase and throw in **'spiders'** and **'mars'** as additional but separate search terms. Our hit rate jumped from 2 to 8 when we tried this. We also suspected that the album might be described by some simply as 'Ziggy Stardust' so we tried dropping 'spiders' and 'mars', which gave us 79 promising results.

Quotation marks bind search terms as inseparable phrases.

Home > All Categories > **Search Results for '"ziggy stardust" ...'**

All Items	**Auctions**	**Buy It Now**

"ziggy stardust" spiders mars   All Categories ▾   Search Advanced Search
☐ Search title **and** description

Matching Categories | 8 items found for **"ziggy stardust" spiders mars**

Exclude key words

We saw above how to exclude certain terms from a search with a minus sign so just a note here. Be very careful indeed when trying to exclude common key terms like 'used' or 'second hand' (or '2nd hand'). The risk is twofold. First, experienced eBayers will often avoid using such terms so that their items show up in your searches regardless. For instance, an old Gameboy might be described as 'seldom-played', 'one careful owner' or 'in new condition' rather than as 'used'. Secondly, if you exclude 'used' as a search term, you will miss perfectly innocent descriptions like 'new, not used' and 'never been used'.

Search within results

Rather than trying to narrow a search from the outset with the concomitant risk of filtering out perfectly valid hits, you can start with fairly broad criteria and then search *within* the results. For instance, a search on **eminem 8 mile** might throw up 85 items. The sidebar on the left-hand side of the results page then shows you how these hits are dispersed throughout various eBay categories. In this example, 36 of the hits are located in the DVD category and 7 in CDs, which is a useful way of rooting out movies from movie soundtracks.

Let's say that you want a DVD but suddenly remember the significance of region coding. A DVD produced for the Region 1 (US) market will not play on a standard Region 2 (UK) DVD player (unless the player is specifically billed as multiregional). Click DVDs in the sidebar and then either *add* 'region 2' to the search criteria or *exclude* 'region 1' to narrow the search to suitable items. At this point, we would suggest that you broaden your search to titles and description, as region coding information is likely to be buried in the small print.

One further point. In the example above where we had 79 hits for 'ziggy stardust', we could add 'cd' as a search term to theoretically narrow the results to music alone, thereby excluding Ziggy the Movie DVDs or Ziggy-related books. Doing this reduced our hits from 79 to 22. However, we could instead click the CD category, in which case we would have 43 hits. This sounds odd but the reason is that several items were described along the lines of: 'David Bowie's Ziggy Stardust album digitally remastered with bonus tracks'. That is, with no mention of 'CD' anywhere in the title or description. You might call this carelessness on the part of the seller but it's important to factor in such omissions nevertheless.

This method of searching for key words first and then narrowing the search to specific categories is our favoured approach.

Use the Matching Categories sidebar to refine your hits.

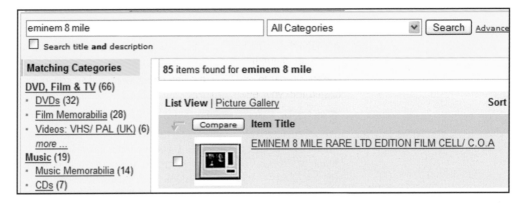

Here we have added 'region 2' to the search field within the DVDs category. Note that we are also broadening the search to include descriptions.

Misspellings

A small point, perhaps, but an important one. People often make spelling mistakes and the eBay search engine is not smart enough to work around them on your behalf. For instance, we would strongly suggest an either/or search for **(eminem,eminnem,emminem,emminnemm,enimmen,emimem, mnm)** rather than searching for **eminem** alone. Indeed, you might even stumble upon an auction that nobody else has noticed precisely because they haven't covered all spelling variations.

To prove the point, we searched for:

(eminnem,emminem,emminnemm,enimmen,emimem,mnm) - eminem

The idea was to exclude all items in which Eminem's name was spelled correctly and find only the mistakes. The result? One pair of 'SZ 12 EMIMEM SHINY DENIM JEANS'. Ah well, it just might have been an ultra-rare signed gold disk.

Have a look at **http://fatfingers.co.uk** for an automated approach to finding mis-spelled search terms.

Location, location, location

By default, eBay will only show you items being sold from within your own country. However, it's perfectly possible, even likely, that there are overseas sellers out there who are only too happy to ship a CD (although not, perhaps, a wardrobe) to the UK. To uncover them, initiate a search and then click the Refine Search link next to the Search button. In the Location section, turn on the Items available to UK option.

Not much to rap about this time around but searching for mis-spelled listings can bag you a bargain.

Save your searches

Finally for now, eBay provides a handy way of saving a search so that you can repeat it in the future. This is well worth investigating if:

● You tend to buy the same items time and time again.

● Your first search draws a blank.

● You find a suitable item but lose out in the auction and want to find an alternative.

Here's what to do. Note that you can only save a search when logged into your eBay account.

Conduct your search in the normal manner, applying as many of the above techniques as you like. Now click the Add to Favourites link at the top of the search results page.

2

Up pops a screen with a summary of your search criteria and an invitation to give it a more memorable name. Your search is then automatically saved in your My eBay page. More about My eBay later (p84).

Add to My Favourite Searches

Search Criteria

Items matching '"ziggy stardust" spiders mars -dvd'
Sort: Ending Soonest

Search Name
"ziggy stardust" spiders mars
30 characters maximum

3

There is an additional option to receive daily email notifications from eBay for a period of between a week and a year. What happens is that eBay automatically runs your search for you once a day and lets you know whenever a new item is listed.

Search Name
Ziggy search
30 characters maximum

☑ Email me daily whenever there are new items for [6 months ▼]
Email notifications are a convenient way to see n... e interested in.

| 7 days |
| 14 days |
| 1 month |
| 2 months |
| 3 months |
| 6 months |
| 12 months |

[Save Search] Cancel

4

At any time, you can open My eBay by following the link at the top of every eBay page. Look for the All Favourites heading in the left-hand sidebar, and a subheading called Searches. Click this.

All Selling
■ Scheduled
■ Selling
■ Sold (1)
■ Unsold (1)

All Favourites
■ Searches
■ Sellers
■ Categories

[Delete]

How to Use Favourite

① Search for your ite
Search for an item o

② Click on the "Add t
If you are happy with
....

5

Here you will find the search you saved. Click its name to run a fresh search on the current eBay inventory. You can save up to 100 searches at a time and run them as often as you like.

Favourite Searches (1 search; 1 email)   Add new Search

☐ Name of Search △   Search Criteria   Email Settings   Action

☐ Ziggy search   "ziggy stardust" spiders mars -dvd   180 days left   Edit
                            Sort: Ending Soonest   Preferences

[Delete]   Search items will be emailed to: ebay@scunnered.com

                                                                                    Back to top

PART  Feeling your way around feedback

Feedback is the lifeblood of eBay. In a community based more on trust than legislation, it is the means by which buyers and sellers make informed decisions about who to deal with and who to avoid. It is actually a very simple system indeed, but one that you must understand before making a purchase or a sale.

In essence, each of the two parties involved in an eBay transaction leaves comments about the other. When a seller receives prompt payment, he says so; and when a buyer receives his goods in time, and as described, properly packaged and intact, he returns the compliment. As a happy buyer, you might say: 'Great product, just as described. Seller answered my emails promptly'. As a seller, your comment might be along the lines of, 'Top communication and immediate payment. If only all eBayers were as reliable! A+++.'

These reciprocal comments – feedback – are published on the eBay website and are publicly available to anyone, member or non-member. The idea is that you check a trader's feedback before entering into an auction transaction.

Every sale you make or item you buy is listed in your public feedback profile. So too are all the things that fellow traders say about you.

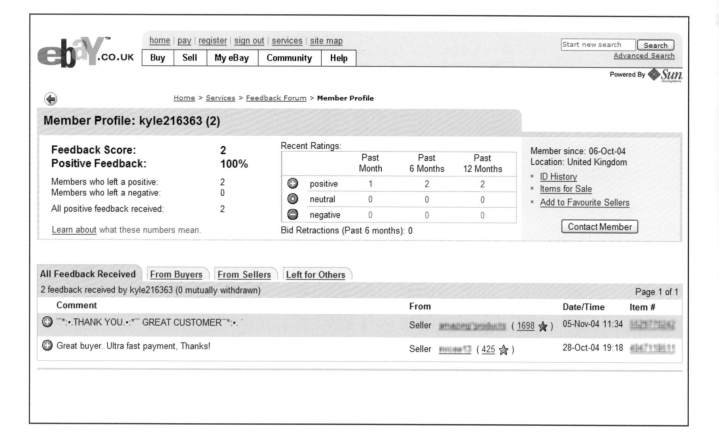

To give and to receive

Feedback takes the form of a freeform comment (limited to 80 characters) but rather more important than the actual wording is the type of feedback that you leave. There are three choices: positive, neutral and negative. As a golden rule, you leave positive feedback whenever you are happy with the transaction. You may wish to temper your enthusiasm with a word or two in the freeform comment – 'Delivery could perhaps have been swifter' – but bear in mind that hardly anybody will ever read it.

Let's say you sell a perfectly good first edition of a valuable book. The buyer pays up and you ship the book. A day or so goes by and then you receive a politely worded message from the buyer:

'Thank you for item number 12345, which I received today. However, I was a little disappointed to find that the book was not quite as described. There is some light staining on the back of the dust jacket, some pages have been folded down at the corner, and page 113 has a small tear. The overall yellowing of the pages is also more significant than was evident from your photograph or description.'

Now, several things may happen at this point:

● You get on your high horse, email back that you've never heard such rubbish and promise never to deal with him again.

● You bite you lip, realise that he has a point, but ignore the message. After all, you've been paid…

● You reply in conciliatory mode and express your concern about his disappointment. What would he consider to be a fair way forward?

How or indeed whether you resolve this query is important for your future business on eBay because your response now is likely to determine what kind of feedback the buyer leaves. If you reply in anger, he would be quite entitled to leave negative

The Feedback Forum – http://pages.eBay.co.uk/services/forum/feedback.html – is well worth a browse before you leave your first feedback.

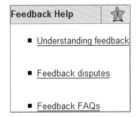

Feedback

Enter an eBay User ID   [   ] [Find Member]

Welcome to the Feedback Forum
The Feedback Forum is the place to learn about your trading partners, view their reputations, and express your opinions by leaving feedback on your transactions. Such member-to-member comments help the millions of buyers and sellers in the community build trust and share their trading experiences with others.

Useful Links		Feedback Help	
■ **Leave feedback**	■ Reply to feedback received	■ Understanding feedback	
■ **View my Member Profile**	■ Follow up to feedback left	■ Feedback disputes	
	■ Hide my feedback	■ Feedback FAQs	

How to use the Feedback Forum
Every eBay member has a profile in the Feedback Forum. A profile has basic information about the member and a list of feedback left by their trading partners from previous transactions. Learning to trust a member of the community has a lot to do with what their past customers or sellers have to say!

feedback. Surprisingly, perhaps, a regular trader is actually unlikely to do so. Negative feedback tends to be reserved for downright crooks and is regarded on eBay as a deeply serious matter. In this example, you've merely oversold an item and rudely responded to an enquiry. You might get negative feedback but you're more likely to 'escape' with a neutral comment.

If you ignore the enquiry, neutral feedback is again a possibility but it's perhaps more likely that you'll receive no feedback at all. Withholding feedback is itself a mild form of retribution in the curious world of eBay. You would be very unlikely to get stung with negative feedback unless the buyer was desperately unhappy with his purchase, but you would be equally unlikely to find him bidding on one of your future auctions.

In the third case where you show willing, you would almost certainly be rewarded with positive feedback. In fact, the buyer might not press for a refund or even a discount. It is to the advantage of all concerned that eBay traders abide by the spirit of the game and one of the cardinal tenets is that items should be described precisely. In this example, the buyer may simply be trying to point this out to you in the hope that you'll take it on board for the future. In other words, he'll live with a small personal disappointment for the sake of the greater good.

Does that sound fantastically idealistic? That's eBay for you.

Feedback is a powerful check against shoddy or fraudulent trading. Ignore it at your peril.

⊕ fast delivery and problem free...recommended!	Buyer
◉ delivery time poor, wrong item delivered, further delay - wont be using again!	Buyer
⊕ Many thanks - excellent service - recommended.	Buyer
⊖ prompt delivery but it just wont work!	Buyer
⊕ Excellent communication, quick transaction, Excellent deal, very very pleased	Buyer

Feedback scores and ratings

A feedback profile has two parts: a *feedback score* and a *positive feedback rating*. To understand how it works, imagine the following scenario in which Bob trades on eBay 100 times:

- 86 people leave positive feedback (86 points).
- 3 leave neutral feedback (0 points).
- 2 leave negative feedback (-2 points).
- 9 leave no feedback (0 points).

Bob's feedback score is a simple total of his total positive feedback points after deducting the negatives. Here, this gives a score of 84. This number appears next to Bob's User ID whenever he places a bid or lists an item.

Bob can receive feedback more than once from the same trader providing each is for a separate transaction. However, multiple feedbacks from the same trader do not count more than once towards his feedback score. This is to stop high scores being generated by transactions with only a small number of specific traders (perhaps friends). The general rule is: one trader, one score.

In the above example, we might suppose the same eBayer bought three items from Bob in three separate auctions, and left positive feedback each time. eBay would then automatically strip out the two duplicates and reduce Bob's feedback score to 82 (of his tally of 86 positive points, three are from the same trader and only one counts).

A feedback score is an at-a-glance way of letting other eBayers know how long you have been around. However, by itself it doesn't tell the whole story. It doesn't even tell the important part of the story.

Bob's positive feedback rating is the real key to his trustworthiness on eBay. This is his total positive feedback points as a percentage of the total feedback received (both positive and negative), again excluding multiple feedbacks from the same trader. In our original example, Bob's rating would be:

$$86/(86+2) = 97.73\% \text{ (shown simply as 97.7\%)}$$

In our modified example where three of Bob's positives came from the same trader, his rating would be:

$$84/(84+2) = 97.67\% \text{ (shown simply as 97.7\%)}$$

We can see here that there's a slight advantage for Bob in the first scenario where he has no repeat customers. In a sense, this reflects reality, for it is, or should be, easier to do business with the same people repeatedly than with new customers every time. Arguably, the difference in feedback score is not marked enough.

If we extend this example and suppose that of Bob's 86 positive feedbacks no fewer than 40 come from the same regular trader – not so very unlikely on eBay – then the sum becomes:

$$47/(47+2) = 95.92 \text{ (shown simply as 95.9\%)}$$

Bob still looks like a very safe, reliable trader with a positive feedback rating of 95.9% but that's almost 2 points off the 97.7% he could have if every trade had been with a unique user. In other words, the more widely you trade, the higher your feedback rating. And if you thought you and a friend could set up eBay accounts and build high feedback scores by trading with one another relentlessly, think again.

In this example, the eBayer has received a total of 17,354 positive feedbacks from 11,053 unique members. He has also received 21 negatives from unique members. His feedback score is thus his total unique positives less his total unique negatives i.e. 11,053 – 21 = 11,032. His positive feedback rating is his total unique positives as a percentage of his total unique feedback i.e. 11,053 as a percentage of 11,074 equals 99.8%. This is the really important figure.

Member Profile:		(11032 ☆)	Power Seller		

Feedback Score:	11032
Positive Feedback:	99.8%
Members who left a positive:	11053
Members who left a negative:	21
All positive feedback received:	17354

Learn about what these numbers mean.

Recent Ratings:

		Past Month	Past 6 Months	Past 12 Months
⊕	positive	837	4618	10061
◎	neutral	2	12	18
⊖	negative	2	5	15

Bid Retractions (Past 6 months): 0

Feedback summarised

There's no escaping feedback on eBay but as so often the trick is understanding what's going on and making the system work to your advantage. Some further thoughts:

● The more you trade, the more likely you are to have a one-off deal that goes bad and results in negative feedback. That's simply inevitable. However, the more you trade, the less important the odd negative feedback becomes. Remember, your positive feedback rating is a percentage.

● If one deal in your first five results in a negative, your positive feedback rating would be 80% (four positives as a percentage of five total feedbacks received). In the real world, 80% is a respectable score. But in eBay, you will struggle to sell anything to anybody with that kind of rating. You will also find many sellers unprepared to accept your bids. This is one reason why it is so important to appreciate the importance of feedback – and to use negative feedback only in extreme circumstances. You may feel slightly short-changed by a transaction but, unless you are absolutely convinced that the other party was out to rip you off, you should not resort to negative feedback. It's akin to daubing 'Rip-off Merchant' in bright red paint on a high street shop's window.

● Some eBay traders never leave feedback. You can certainly request that they do – and the eBay system itself sends gentle reminders – but there's no necessity to do so. This can be galling, particularly when you're anxious to build up a favourable feedback rating, but those are the breaks.

eBay feedback is for life, not just the heat of the moment, so be careful what you write.

● Deciding when to leave feedback is a tricky matter. Let's say you're the seller. An eBayer wins your auction and sends you

---

Home > Services > Feedback Forum > **Leave Feedback**

Feedback Forum: Leave Feedback
help

Every eBay user has a feedback score based on ratings from other members. Feedback lets you reward eBay users and inform the community about your experiences with others. Typically, members give a positive rating if they are happy with a transaction, and a negative when basic obligations have not been met. Keep in mind that what you say about other members becomes a permanent part of their eBay reputation.

Please note:
- ◆ Once left, you cannot edit or retract feedback; you are solely responsible for the content.
- ◆ It's always best to keep your feedback factual; avoid making personal remarks.
- ◆ Feedback can be left for at least 90 days following a transaction.
- ◆ If you have a dispute, contact your trading partner to try and resolve the dispute before leaving feedback.

User ID: slightly_iffy_trader   Show all transactions

Item Number: 5147922049

Rating: ○ Positive ◉ Neutral ○ Negative ○ I will leave feedback later

Comment: Not in quite the 'as new' condition described in the auction! Buyer beware... | 80 chars max.

[Leave Feedback]

immediate payment, and you ship off the goods. At this point, your side of the deal is seemingly over and you may well be tempted to leave immediate feedback. But what if the buyer falsely claims non-delivery, or demands a refund or replacement on spurious grounds? You might now regret that you were so generous, but you can't change your feedback after the event. Worse, the buyer may unjustly blight your record with a negative and you would have no way to respond in kind. On the community level, you have signalled to all and sundry that this is a trustworthy buyer, whereas the reality is that he's proven to be a cheating, conniving charlatan.

It is thus better to delay seller feedback until both parties are satisfied. Likewise, you should never leave buyer feedback until you have received the goods and checked that they are exactly as expected.

● If you receive a negative comment, all is not necessarily lost. You have a right of reply. If you act in haste and place a negative feedback that you later regret, you can and should modify your comment with an addendum. Better still, you can withdraw your comment if the other party agrees. Note, however, that feedback can not be directly edited or removed. See p114-117 for more on all of this.

Icons and stars

eBay rewards frequent traders with a star system, the idea being that buyers and sellers can see at a glance that you've been around and trading for a while and are thus, presumably, to be trusted. By a similar token, eBay flags new users with a New User icon that highlights your inexperience.

Stars are with you forever, changing as you gain a healthier feedback profile, but your new user ID drops off after 30 days. However, should you change your User ID – something which you can't do within the first 30 days – you'll be lumbered with a changed ID icon for the following month. This serves as a potent warning to all other eBayer that perhaps, just perhaps, you have something to hide.

Hello, kyle216363 (0) ⚐

    Hello, kyle216363 (0) 🐦

eBay flags newcomer status (top) or a changed user ID with icons.

As your positive feedback grows, your status is rewarded with new stars.

The Star Chart

Stars are awarded for achieving a particular Feedback Profile.

- A "Yellow Star" (☆) represents a Feedback Profile of 10 to 49.
- A "Blue Star" (★) represents a Feedback Profile of 50 to 99.
- A "Turquoise Star" (☆) represents a Feedback Profile of 100 to 499.
- A "Purple Star" (☆) represents a Feedback Profile of 500 to 999.
- A "Red Star" (★) represents a Feedback Profile of 1,000 to 4,999.
- A "Green Star" (☆) represents a Feedback Profile of 5,000 to 9,999.
- A "Yellow Shooting Star" (🌠) represents a Feedback Profile of 10,000 to 24,999.
- A "Turquoise Shooting Star" (🌠) represents a Feedback Profile of 25,000 to 49,999.
- A "Purple Shooting Star" (🌠) represents a Feedback Profile of 50,000 to 99,999.
- A "Red Shooting Star" (🌠) represents a Feedback Profile of 100,000 or higher.

Exploring a seller's feedback

Let's locate an eBay auction item and find out a little more about the seller. We'll use a real, random example here but mask the trader's name to protect his privacy. Today, we're in the market for a Gameboy Advance SP (a handheld games console).

Log in to eBay via the home page and conduct a search. When you have a page or more of hits, arrange them however you like (see p37). We're in a hurry so we'll look at auctions in terms of how soon they will close.

Here's a Gameboy with a couple of hours left on the clock, currently priced at £21. There have already been 11 bids which tells us that at least two other people have been sufficiently interested in the item to get involved in a bidding war. This is not to imply that an item without any bids should be disregarded, of course – but you'd want to read the description carefully.

Click the item link to learn more. This opens up a separate page dedicated to this particular auction. To the right are the all-important seller details. Here we see a useful tell-tale icon (well, useful if you can remember what they all mean – see p50 for details) and the seller's positive feedback rating. In this case, it's 100%. Click the User ID or the feedback score to see more.

This eBayer's feedback score is 88 but a total of 96 positives have been received. We can thus deduce that eight of these feedbacks were 'duplicates', where the same trader left feedback more than once. The table shows the breakdown of feedback over time.

Lower down the page, you can view freeform feedback comments. Concentrate on buyers' feedback for now, as this is more relevant when you're considering a bid. You can often glean much about the trader's speed of response, packaging, openness to communication and general attitude. Click any link in the Item column to see what the trader has been buying and selling recently. Your trading record is a matter of public knowledge on eBay.

All Feedback Received	From Buyers	From Sellers	Left for Others	
96 feedback received by ███ (0 mutually withdrawn)				
Comment				**From**
🟢 great buy ! speedy delivery ! thankyou				Buyer
🟢 very fast service would buy from them again				Buyer
🟢 A++ swift payment. Good transaction.				Seller
🟢 1st class ebayer well recommended A+++++++++++++++++++++++++				Buyer

Open the Left for Others page to get an idea of what feedback to expect from this trader if you go ahead and win the auction. Here we see that he has left 103 results compared to 96 received. This is a good sign as it indicates that he is likely to leave you feedback should you win his auction. You need all the feedback you can get on eBay.

All Feedback Received	From Buyers	From Sellers	**Left for Others**	
103 feedback left by ███ (0 mutually withdrawn)				
Comment				**Left Fo**
🟢 Excellent Ebayer. Fast Payment. Thanks a lot.				Buyer
🟢 Excellent Ebayer. Fast Payer. Thanks a lot.				Buyer
🟢 Excellent Ebayer. Fast payment. Thanks a lot.				Buyer
🟢 Brilliant scarf. received safely. Thanks a lot.				Seller

Now click the Items for Sale link to see what else this user is currently selling. Again, this can be constructive: you might discover that he has 50 other Gameboys on offer, which would tell you that he's a serious trader rather than an individual clearing out his attic.

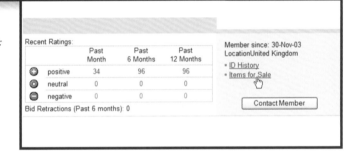

Recent Ratings:	Past Month	Past 6 Months	Past 12 Months	Member since: 30-Nov-03 LocationUnited Kingdom
⊕ positive	34	96	96	▪ ID History
⊙ neutral	0	0	0	▪ Items for Sale
⊖ negative	0	0	0	
Bid Retractions (Past 6 months): 0				Contact Member

This current example is pretty straightforward. The user has traded on eBay more than 100 times, received nearly as many feedbacks as he has left feedback for others – which suggests that people are happy to reciprocate rather than withhold comment – and all of them are positive. He hasn't changed User ID recently and shows all the signs of being a good eBayer. We would feel confident about placing a bid and doing a deal. Click the Back to your last item link to return to the auction.

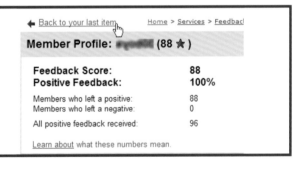

◄ Back to your last item   Home > Services > Feedbac|

Member Profile: ███ (88 ★)

Feedback Score:	**88**
Positive Feedback:	**100%**
Members who left a positive:	88
Members who left a negative:	0
All positive feedback received:	96

Learn about what these numbers mean.

Here's an alternative trader with an altogether different feedback profile. The feedback rating is a seemingly healthy 96.9% but you can see that there have been 5 negatives. Given what we have said about the reluctance with which negatives are dished out in eBay, these certainly repay exploration – especially when we factor in the recently changed User ID (see icon).

◄ Back to your last item   Home > Services > Feedback Forum > Member Profile

Member Profile: sclarkesimports (153 ☆) 🔄

Feedback Score:	**153**	Recent Ratings:	Past Month	Past 6 Months	Past 12 Months
Positive Feedback:	**96.9%**				
Members who left a positive:	158	⊕ positive	80	174	174
Members who left a negative:	5	⊙ neutral	0	1	1
All positive feedback received:	174	⊖ negative	2	5	5
Learn about what these numbers mean.		Bid Retractions (Past 6 months): 0			

By scrolling through the feedback pages, you can identify and read freeform comments attached to negative feedback. This trader has used his right to reply and used it robustly. This right is open to all who receive negative feedback, as we shall see on p116. But who's telling the truth?

⊕ goods as offered - excellent service +++++++++++++++++++++++	Buyer	▓▓▓ (16 ☆)
⊖ given bad reply for no payment, cancelled due to money problem	Buyer	▓▓▓ (23 ☆)
Reply by ▓▓▓: YOU DIDNT EVEN CONTACT ME TO CANCEL YOU IGNORED REMINDERS SELLERS BEWARE!!!!!		
⊕ Fantastic, great to deal with, arrived in time for B'day gift for son A++++++	Buyer	▓▓▓ (9)
⊕ goods as described, satisfied customer, delivery as stated	Buyer	▓▓▓ (19 ☆)

Here's another comment where we can see that a disgruntled buyer has qualified his initial negative feedback with a follow-up response. This is another right (see p116). By reading some of the positives as well as the negatives and by clicking on item links, we

learn that this seller specialises in Gameboys. The overwhelming majority are happy with his service, but a few are not. Would you bid at one of his auctions? We would certainly hesitate, especially when the same item is so readily available elsewhere.

⊖ sent money no product sent no reply to emails oh dear!	Buyer	▓▓▓ (6)
Reply by ▓▓▓: U LEFT FEEDBACK B4 I GOT UR EMAIL.DID REPLY TO EMAIL STRAIGHT AWAY		
Follow-up by ▓▓▓: tried to contact had no reply took nearly 5 weeks to recieve item.ok in end.		

Here's an interesting feedback comment where a buyer has tempered positive feedback to a seller with a comment about postage costs. If we are to believe what

we see here, the seller then hit back with negative feedback and the buyer has returned to warn others of his behaviour. Let's check. Click the buyer's User ID to access his feedback profile.

⊕ Item in good order. Postage charges could have been less, though.	Buyer	▓▓▓ (171 ☆)
Reply by ▓▓▓: The postage was fair, it was very well packaged and sent by recorded delivery.		
Follow-up by ▓▓▓: THIS GUY LEAVES NEG FEEDBACK IF YOU QUERY HIS COSTS - AVOID!!!		

Sure enough, a little browsing reveals the negative feedback from the seller. The buyer has responded rather rudely and the seller has countered his comment. That's the end of the matter. All in all, it's a

minor spat between two traders but it serves to illustrate the importance of feedback. It also shows why it's important to read comments rather than simply avoiding traders with any negative feedback.

⊖ A difficult buyer - read the auction before you bid in future please.	Seller	▓▓▓ (748 ☆)
Reply by ▓▓▓: I paid immediately and left a +ve comment, should I kiss your feet too?		
Follow-up by ▓▓▓: No, try and be a little less rude in future and read the terms BEFORE bidding		

When you know how to search for items and research a seller's feedback, you're just about ready to bid on an eBay auction. But don't press that big Bid Now button quite yet. There remains the question of how you're going to pay for something you win. And that, unfortunately, is a thorny issue. On to Part 3 ...

Current bid:	**£6.01**
	[Place Bid >]
Time left:	**49 mins 13 secs**
	10-day listing
	Ends 30-Nov-04 16:41:23 GMT

PART 3

The ins and outs of PayPal

THE INS AND OUTS OF PAYPAL

Panacea or a necessary evil?

You can't go far in eBay without stumbling upon the ubiquitous PayPal logo. PayPal is a company owned by eBay that facilitates financial transactions between traders. At its simplest, you can use a PayPal account to:

● Pay a seller for an item won at an eBay auction.
● Receive money from a buyer at one of your own auctions.

PayPal integrates into the eBay site with direct links, as we shall see, so it's relatively straightforward to use once you get your account set up.

You can fund a PayPal account in three ways: by direct debit from your bank account; with a credit card; or by accepting PayPal payments from other eBayers. You can then use these funds to pay anybody else who has a PayPal account.

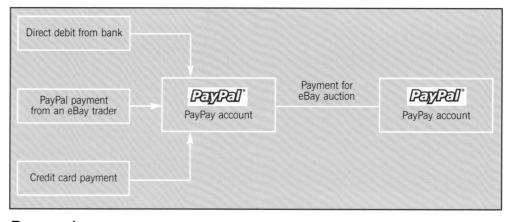

Pros and cons

In a perfect world, any two parties would be able to exchange money immediately and freely. In a less perfect world, we would all be able to make and, crucially, take credit card payments. But the fact is that sending money to and receiving money from other people is something of a fiddle.

As a buyer, you can send a cheque, postal order or international money order, but in virtually all cases the seller will wait for the funds to clear before shipping your goods. You can send cash in the post, but you'd be a fool to do so. You could arrange a direct bank transfer but you'll have no comeback whatsoever if the seller proves to be a fraud. What you would probably like to do is pay by credit card – payment is instant and you have built-in fraud protection with your credit card issuer – but most sellers have no means of taking credit card payments. This usually requires full-blown merchant status, whereas most eBayers are individuals.

As a seller, you want to be paid for your item as quickly as possible. You probably don't want to visit the bank, fill out a paying-in slip and stand in line. Prudence dictates that you wait for a cheque to clear before shipping the item won at auction – it's the only sensible policy – but this means checking with your bank and a separate outing to the post office. It can also interfere with holiday plans and generally adds to clutter around the home.

PayPal or bust

This is why PayPal is so popular. Payment is immediate and relatively secure, and anybody can send money to anybody else. Such is its dominance on eBay that many sellers now accept only PayPal for payment. Although this is seemingly counter-productive, they know that there are sufficient PayPal account holders out there to win every auction so they're prepared to live without business from non-PayPal users. The first time you come upon an auction for an item that you really, really want and discover that it's PayPal or nothing, you'll be strongly tempted to sign up.

It's also the case that you'll put off a great many potential bidders unless you accept PayPal as payment for your own auctions. Of course, it's possible to accept cheques or postal orders alongside PayPal so it's not necessarily an exclusive either/or equation. Many sellers say they prefer PayPal but they're prepared to accept other forms of payment. This, we suggest, is the most sensible position to adopt as a seller.

Just to be clear about one thing here: payment terms on eBay are entirely a matter for the seller. When you list an item, you stipulate clearly how you wish to be paid and any bidder is bound by those terms. If you say you'll accept only a personal cheque or postal order, then the buyer has no right to ask you to take a PayPal payment (although some will certainly try). If you say the sale is PayPal only, then that too is fine.

The main advantage to PayPal is thus double-handed: with a PayPal account you can buy from and sell to the widest possible audience. You can also send and receive payments in different currencies (at a cost of 2.5% over and above the current exchange rate), which is an obvious boon for trading internationally.

Payment methods accepted

This seller, ▓▓▓▓ , prefers PayPal.

• **PayPal**® (MasterCard VISA AMEX ⑤ ⑥ ▢▢▢ VISA Electron)
• Personal cheque
• Other - See Payment Instructions for payment methods accepted

Learn about payment methods.

Many sellers accept *only* PayPal for eBay auctions but others, like this one, remain more flexible.

Payment methods accepted

• Personal cheque
• Postal Order or Banker's Draft
• Other - See Payment Instructions for payment methods accepted

Learn about payment methods.

Auctions which don't accept PayPal at all are increasingly rare.

Fees and freeze

Unfortunately, PayPal is not entirely free. However, transaction fees are levied on sellers, not buyers, so you can at least get started without incurring any charges. We also feel that PayPal's fees are reasonable on the whole and a fair price to pay for the undoubted convenience. We'll look at these as we go along. Think of PayPal as an optional cost of doing business on eBay.

Far more concerning is the PayPal User Agreement. You'll find this by clicking the User Agreement link at the bottom of PayPal UK's home page: **www.paypal.com/uk**. Be warned: this is a mammoth document studded with hyperlinks to further information. The area that concerns us and many others most is that PayPal has the right to freeze, or 'limit', any account for up to 180 days for pretty much any reason it likes. If you have money sitting in that account, you can't withdraw it.

You'll find a list of specific reasons why PayPal might freeze your account by following the Closing Accounts and Limiting Account Access link on the User Agreement web page. It includes such wide-ranging nuggets as:

● Complaints received regarding non-dispatch of merchandise, non-delivery of services, merchandise not as described, or problems with merchandise sent (i.e. an eBay user with a grudge could get your PayPal account frozen).

● Receipt of potentially fraudulent funds (even if you have no way of knowing).

● Breach of this User Agreement (which means, among other things, that PayPal can freeze your account for listing on eBay what it considers to be sexually-oriented goods or services, or anything to do with drugs or gambling). You can also be fined £250 for listing inappropriate items.

Now, we're not saying that PayPal doesn't have the right to operate whatever terms and conditions it sees fit. If you sign up to the service, you agree to be bound to those terms and have little cause for complaint. However, there is considerable ill-will towards PayPal from people who consider that they have been treated unfairly and in some cases had their money 'stolen'. We point this out merely so you are aware that it is not necessarily plain sailing all the way with PayPal. To find out more, have a browse at the charmingly named PayPal Sucks website: **www.paypalsucks.com**.

Another User Agreement to read, understand and take on board. Always remember that PayPal has access to your money so a relationship is not to be entered into lightly.

PART  # Types of PayPal account

There are currently three types of PayPal account:

Personal Account This is the starting point and fine for most purposes. With a personal account, you can spend up to £500. You can also receive any amount into your account but you may only withdraw up to £500 per month for the first three months. In order to spend and withdraw larger amounts, you must 'verify' your account (see p66-67).

Crucially, though, you can not receive payments where the sender uses a credit card. If this happens, you have to either refuse the payment or upgrade to a Premier account. If you sell on eBay, you'll probably need to accept credit card payments through PayPal at some point, if only because buyers expect to be able to use them.

No fees are charged when you send or receive money with a Personal account. However, you are charged 25p every time you withdraw funds of under £50 from your PayPal account i.e. transfer money received to your bank account. Withdrawals of £50 or over are free.

Premier Account The main difference here is that you can accept credit card payments. That is, a buyer can use his credit card via his PayPal account to make a payment into your PayPal account. However, here you have to pay a fee. As we write, this stands at 3.4% of the total transaction plus 20p (although it gets progressively cheaper with single transactions in excess of £1,500, £6,000 and £15,000). These fees apply to *every* transaction when you have a Premier account, *not just those made with a credit card*. The same cash withdrawal fees apply here as with a Personal account.

Most people sign up for a Personal PayPal account first, verifying it only if and when they need to increase their receiving limit or when somebody tries to make a credit card-funded payment and forces their hand. However, we suggest that it's easier to bite the PayPal bullet right from the outset by going straight for a Premier account. It will increase your cost of selling items on eBay by that 3.4% plus 20p per transaction, but will also make life easier in the long run.

As a *buyer*, there are no extra fees to pay by opening a Premier account.

Business Account The same as a Premier account, essentially, but you can trade under a business name rather than your own.

PayPal fees

	Personal account	Premier account
Make a payment	Free	Free
Receive a payment	Free	3.4% of the total eBay transaction (up to £1,500) plus 20p
Withdraw funds from PayPal account to bank account	Free for withdrawals over £50; otherwise 25p	Free for withdrawals over £50; otherwise 25p

PART **5** # Registering with PayPal

We set up a brand new eBay account earlier. We have to
make a bid or list an item but now is as good a time as
any to go live with PayPal. This way, you'll be prepared
to win your first auction even if it's a PayPal-only listing.

Sign in to your eBay account at the eBay home page:
www.ebay.co.uk. Towards the bottom of the left-hand
sidebar, look for the PayPal link. As we remarked earlier,
PayPal is tightly integrated with eBay (not least because
eBay owns PayPal and has a clear, nay naked, interest
in promoting it).

Related Links

PayPal 📴

Buyer's Guide

Shop eBay Shop

Search for Items

Dispute Resolution

Report a Problem

Unpaid Item Disputes

Spend some time on this page browsing the tutorials
and try to get a handle on how PayPal works – which is
not altogether obvious. Then click one of the PayPal
links to go straight to the registration page. You can also
go directly to **www.paypal.com/uk** and use the Sign Up
button.

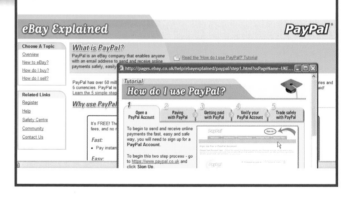

Your first choice is between a Personal or a Business
account, which is a tad confusing given what we said
above about the three distinct types of PayPal account.
No matter, select Personal and see Step 5. Tell PayPal
where you live.

4

Now complete the registration form in full. We suggest that you use the same email address here as you did when you signed up with eBay on p29. However, it's sensible to use a different password, and indeed one that is unique to this site rather than one you use generally. PayPal links to your bank account and anybody with knowledge of your password could conceivably steal your money. Make it a good, secure password and don't write it down anywhere.

5

Towards the end of the form, you'll find an innocuous Premier account upgrade option. If you haven't already read through PayPal's terms and conditions or the opening material in this section of the book, let us reiterate here that a Premier account will allow you to take credit card payments from eBay buyers and cost you a small fee on each and every transaction. We decided to upgrade. Complete the form and click the Sign Up button.

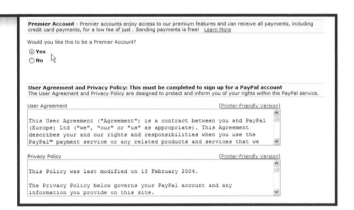

6

The next stage in the process is to check the email account you registered in Step 4 for a message from PayPal and click the link contained in it. This fires up a web page where you'll be asked to enter your password. From PayPal's perspective, this procedure 'confirms' your email address. You can now use the Continue button on the confirmation web page to access your account.

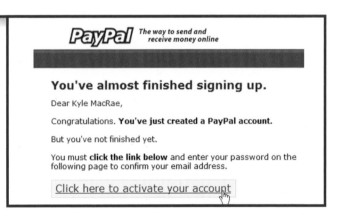

7

You can also log into your account at any time directly via the PayPal home page at **www.paypal.com/uk**. Open the Overview tab on the My Account page to see your virgin PayPal account in all its glory. If you're left thinking that it's not immediately obvious what to do next, you would be right. Read on...

PART **3** # Exploring PayPal

There are many online services that have you up and running in a jiffy. PayPal is not one of them. What we need to now, apart from a good deal of patience, is a little rooting around the site. Like eBay, only worse, the PayPal Help system borders on the obtuse but here there are no helpful user forums. Let's go exploring.

Continuing immediately on from Step 8 in the previous section, click the View Limits link on the My Account page. At the time of writing, a new Premier account holder can send up to £500 in total and withdraw up to £500 per month up to a maximum of £1,500. However, these limits will be waived if you verify your account. We'll come back to that later (see p66-67).

Sending Limit

Your **Sending Limit** is the maximum amount of money you can send through PayPal before enroling in the Verification Program. We ask users to enrol to increase security for everyone.

Your Sending Limit is: £500.00 GBP

£500.00 GBP Remaining

To lift this limit, please enrol in PayPal's Verification Program.

Learn more about Verification.

2

For now, we'll get a little practice (but don't feel obliged to do this yourself). Click the Send Money tab at the top of the page and ensure that the Pay Anyone tab is open (not the Pay for eBay items tab). Enter a secondary email address if you have one – not the address that you registered with PayPal – or that of a friend. Enter £5 and use the dropdown menu to specify that the payment is for a service. Put something in the title and note fields, and click Continue.

| Pay Anyone | Pay for eBay items |

Send Money   Secure Transaction 🔒

Pay anyone with an email address - even if they don't have a PayPal account.

Recipient's Email:

Amount: 5.00   Limit: **£500.00 GBP**   Get Verified to raise limit

Currency: Pounds Sterling ▾ ❓

Type: Service ▾ ❓

Subject: Payment
(optional)

Note: Here's that fiver I owe you
(optional)

3

Suddenly it gets interesting. Right now, before we can continue, we have to register a credit or debit card with PayPal. Of course, the £5 payment has to be funded somehow but PayPal's spectacularly unhelpful Help menu gives no up front warning of this requirement.

⚠ To send money instantly, please add a credit card or debit card to your account.

Add Credit Card or Debit Card

American Express cards will be charged in USD. Paying with American Express will result in currency conversion fees if your card is not denominated in USD and/or if you send a non-USD payment.

Debit Cards (also called check cards, ATM cards or banking cards) are accepted if they have a Visa or MasterCard logo.

You have 0 credit or debit cards active on your account.

First Name: Kyle

Last Name: MacRae

Card Type: ▾

Card Number:

Expiry Date: 01 ▾ 2004 ▾

Let's try a different tack. Return to My Account and open the Add Funds tab. Now follow the link that invites you to add funds to your PayPal account. The theory here is that if you have money in your account, you can use it make payments. You can now, if you like, give PayPal details of your bank account and arrange for a money transfer.

| My Account | Send Money | Request Money | Merchant Tools | Auction Tools |
| Overview | Add Funds | Withdraw | History | Resolution Centre | Profile |

Add Funds

You may make payments from your bank account without adding funds to your PayPal balance.

However, if you feel more comfortable knowing that there are funds in your PayPal balance, you may add them now. While waiting for the funds to clear, you may continue using your PayPal account as usual.

If you have a bank account, you will need to initiate a bank transfer through your bank to add funds to your PayPal account.

Options	Processing Time	Cost
Transfer Funds from a Bank Account in the United Kingdom	7-9 Working Days ❓	Free!

Hmm. Having 'added' a bank account, we now find that we must set up a Direct Debit mandate in order to transfer funds into the PayPal account and/or transfer funds from PayPal back to the bank. This is a convoluted process whereby PayPal deposits two small amounts in your account.

You have added a UK bank account!

Set up Direct Debit for the following benefits:

- Make instant payments straight from your bank account
- Add funds from your bank account
- Funds sent from your bank account will not count towards your Sending Limit

Congratulations - You have successfully added your bank or building society details. You may now withdraw funds from your PayPal account into this bank account.

You May Now Set Up Direct Debit

It's Easy to Confirm Your Bank Account!

 PayPal will make two small deposits into your bank account.

 Check your bank statement or call your bank in 3-5 working days to find out the **exact** amounts of these two deposits.

 Log in to your PayPal account, click the **Set Up Direct Debit** link, and enter these amounts.

Click Set up Direct Debit and complete the mandate that instructs your bank to make payments on demand to PayPal. You can now do nothing more until you know the value of the deposits, at which point you must return here to complete the process (see Step 14). In the worst case, you might have to wait until you receive your next bank statement in the post. Ho hum ...

Please confirm all information and submit if correct. If you have any questions, please contact customer service at directdebit@paypal.co.uk.

Originator's Name
PayPal International Ltd.

Originator's Address
PO Box 714
Richmond TW9 1WS
United Kingdom

Instruction to Your Bank or Building Society to Pay by Direct Debit

Name(s) of Account Holder(s)
Kyle MacRae

Originator's Identification Number
6 7 9 8 4 8

Reference Number

Bank/Building Society Account Number

Branch Sort Code

Name and Full Address of Your Bank or Building Society

Name Bank of Scotland

Address 1

Instruction to your bank or building society
Please pay JPMC Re: PayPal International Ltd. Direct Debit from the bank account detailed in this instruction is subject to the safeguards assured by the Direct Debit Guarantee. I understand that this instruction may remain with JPMC Re: PayPal International Ltd. and if so, details will be passed electronically to my Bank/Building Society.

Date: 15/10/2004

Back in Step 2, we were invited to fund PayPal payments by credit card. We'll return to this scenario now on the assumption that it should be quicker than the Direct Debit alternative. From the Overview tab in My Account, click the Add Credit Card link.

This leads to the same (secure, so safe) web page that we saw in Step 3. This time around, we'll complete the form. Again, though, it's worth noting that PayPal doesn't really explain what's going to happen next. This is very much the style of the service: you find out what to do only when it's time to do it. Complete the form and click Add Card.

Add Credit Card or Debit Card

American Express cards will be charged in USD. Paying with American Express will result in currency conversion fees if your card is not denominated in USD and/or if you send a non-USD payment.

Debit Cards (also called check cards, ATM cards or banking cards) are accepted if they have a Visa or MasterCard logo.

You have 0 credit or debit cards active on your account.

First Name: Kyle

Last Name: MacRae

Card Type:

Card Number:

Expiry Date: 01 ▾ 2004 ▾

PayPal 'adds' the card to your account, which should mean that you're able to use it immediately to make a payment. Let's see. Return to Send Money and fill out the form again. And yes indeed – the payment is ready to be made. However, note the warning that 'This recipient is not yet registered'. The problem is that you can only send money to other PayPal account holders, not to 'anyone with an email address' as PayPal optimistically suggests.

Sending Limit

Your **Sending Limit** is the maximum amount of money you can send through PayPal before enroling in the Verification Program. We ask users to enrol to increase security for everyone.

Your Sending Limit is: £500.00 GBP

£500.00 GBP Remaining

To lift this limit, please enrol in PayPal's Verification Program.

Learn more about Verification.

If you click Send Money, the recipient will receive an email from PayPal telling them that there's £5 awaiting collection. It is then up to that person to register with PayPal in order to receive the money. They'll also have to go through the bank account verification procedure described in Steps 5–6 and 14–16 before the money actually hits their bank account. Be aware of this before you offer to pay a non-PayPal user via PayPal: it may be convenient for you but it makes them jump through hoops.

to me

Dear

You've got cash!

Kyle MacRae just sent you money with PayPal.

Payment Details

Amount: 5.00 GBP

Subject: Payment #2

Note:
Here comes the fiver...

Simply click https://www.paypal.com/uk/links/uni and complete PayPal's easy registration form to claim your money.

In this example, we cancel the payment a little later on. This is always an option with PayPal so long as a payment remains unclaimed and the cash has not actually been transferred. The recipient receives a second email to the effect that the transaction has been withdrawn.

Status: Unclaimed

Subject: Payment #2
Note: Here comes the fiver...
Postal Address: Kyle MacRae

United Kingdom
Confirmed Help

Contact Telephone:

Funding Type: Credit Card
Funding Source: £5.00 GBP - Card Visa/Delta/Electron XXXX-XXXX-XXXX-0013
This credit card transaction will appear on your statement as "PayPal Europe LTD".

Need help? If you have problems with a transaction or would like assistance settling a dispute with your seller, visit the Resolution Centre.

Cancel Payment   Return to Log

If you send money to an email address that is already 'linked to' (registered with) a PayPal account, the procedure is much simpler. The recipient merely has to accept payment and the cash appears in their account immediately. But there are two caveats. The first we have already discussed: unless the recipient has already set up a Direct Debit mandate, they can't actually withdraw the funds from their PayPal account. They could use the money to pay for an eBay auction item but that's a long way short of cash in pocket.

PayPal *The way to send and receive money online*

You've got cash!

Dear ,

Kyle MacRae just sent you money with PayPal.

Kyle MacRae is an **Unverified buyer.**

Payment Details

Amount: 5.00 GBP

Transaction ID: 5JM884121U329645F

Subject: Here's the £5 I owe you...

Note: Sorry for the delay

View the details of this transaction online

The second problem is that if you use a credit card to fund a payment to a Personal account holder, they will be unable to collect the payment unless they first upgrade their own account to Premier status (more hoops, and they'll have to pay a fee on this and every subsequent transaction). Again, this puts the onus on the recipient, which they may not appreciate. To make life easier for the seller, you could use cleared funds from your PayPal account, but this means going through the tedious Direct Debit procedure already described. Speaking of which ...

Subject:	Payment #2
Note:	Here comes the fiver...
Postal Address:	Kyle MacRae
	United Kingdom
	Confirmed
Contact Telephone:	
Funding Type:	Credit Card
Funding Source:	£5.00 GBP - Card Visa/Delta/Electron XXXX-XXXX-XXXX-0013

This credit card transaction will appear on your statement as "PayPal Europe LTD".

PayPal's deposits from Step 6 have finally shown up in our bank account so we can return to the My eBay page and follow the My Account/PayPal Account link. From there, click Go to My Account Overview and sign in to PayPal when prompted. Alternatively, you can sign in to PayPal directly from its own home page: **www.paypal.com/uk**.

Mini Statement ▼▲	Date ▼▲	Type ▼▲	▼▲	Amount ▼▲
PAYPAL VERIFY PAYPAL VERIFY BANK	21-10-2004	CDT	0-2004	
PAYPAL VERIFY PAYPAL VERIFY BANK	21-10-2004	CDT	0-2004	

Note the invitation to set up Direct Debit in the Activate Account sidebar. Click this link now, having first made a note of the two small deposits made to your bank account by PayPal.

Activate Account

🏛 Set up direct debit

What's New?

New PayPal (Europe) Ltd. User Agreement

UK Premier Account Overview

Name: Kyle MacRae
Email: _____ (Add email)
Status: UK - Unverified (New)

Balance: £0.00 GBP   View Limits

Enter the two amounts in the form and click Submit. The following page confirms that you can now use Instant Bank Transfer to send money. This means is that you can pay for an eBay auction item via a cash transfer from your bank account to the seller's PayPal account via your own PayPal account. It's an alternative to funding payment with your credit card, and means you can pay somebody who has only a Personal PayPal account (and thus cannot accept credit card-funded payments).

Confirm Your Bank Account and Set Up Direct Debit

In order to set up direct debit, PayPal may have made two small deposits into your bank account. You may have requested these deposits or they may have been made when you registered your bank account.

It typically takes **3-5 working days** for these deposits to appear in your account. Check your bank statement to find out how much was deposited.

By confirming your bank account details, your bank account will become your default payment method for all PayPal transactions.

Paying with your bank account is:

- **Fast** - payments are immediate, direct from your bank account
- **Safe** - payments are secure, with no risk of building up credit card debt
- **Easy** - use the same bank account for making payments and withdrawals

Please enter these amounts **exactly** as they appear on your bank statement:

Bank Account: Bank of Scotland, XXXXXX7800, Deposits Sent 16 Oct. 2004 ▾

Deposit Amounts: £0.___ GBP (two digits)
£0.___ GBP (two digits)

This process confirms that you are the owner of this bank account because only you have access to the deposit amounts sent by PayPal.

Submit   Cancel

Having set up Direct Debit, we can now transfer money to and from our PayPal account. Let's put this to the test. Back on the main PayPal page, click Add Funds. On the next page, click Transfer Funds from a Bank Account in the United Kingdom.

My Account	Send Money	Request Money	Merchant Tools	Auction Tools
Overview	Add Funds	Withdraw	History	Resolution Centre	Profile

Add Funds

You may make payments from your bank account without adding funds to your PayPal balance.

However, if you feel more comfortable knowing that there are funds in your PayPal balance, you may add them now. While waiting for the funds to clear, you may continue using your PayPal account as usual.

If you have a bank account, you will need to initiate a bank transfer through your bank to add funds to your PayPal account.

Options	Processing Time	Cost
Transfer Funds from a Bank Account in the United Kingdom	7-9 Working Days [?]	Free!

Enter the amount that you wish to transfer and click Continue. Check the details in the following page and click Submit. Then do something else for 7–9 days. Eventually, the cash will show up as cleared funds in your PayPal account. You can use this to make payments to other PayPal accounts.

Add Funds by Electronic Funds Transfer   Secure Transaction 🔒

It takes 7-9 working days to electronically transfer funds from your bank account to your PayPal account.

From: Bank of Scotland Current (Confirmed) XXXXXX7800 ▾
Add Bank Account

Amount: £ 25.00 GBP

To: Your Pound Sterling Balance

Need to send money today? Try an eCheque or Instant Bank Transfer! [?]

Continue

You will now, or shortly, have three ways to fund a payment to somebody for an eBay item (or anything else, come to that) with your PayPal account:

- *Your credit card (so long as the recipient has a Premier or Business PayPal account).*
- *A bank transfer (so long as you have set up Direct Debit).*
- *Cash in your PayPal account.*

To select between these sources, use the More Funding Options on the PayPal payment page. We'll see this in action on p93.

Source of Funds

Instant Bank Transfer: £5.00 GBP from Bank of Scotland XXXXXX7800
Back-Up Funding Source: Visa/Delta/Electron XXXX-XXXX-XXXX-0013
More Funding Options

Back in My Account page now. Despite having registered a credit card and set up a Direct Debit arrangement, PayPal still flags our account as 'unverified'. This is rather galling. However, there's an obvious Get Verified link so let's follow it and see what happens.

Activate Account
⌨ Get Verified

What's New?
New PayPal (Europe) Ltd. User Agreement

UK Premier Account Overview

Name: Kyle MacRae
Email: _____ (Add email)
Status: UK - Unverified (New)

Balance: £0.00 GBP   View Limits

Two further steps are required: verifying account information and supplying merchant information. There's no absolute obligation to complete this process but you may prefer to do so, simply in order that sellers see your verified status. As always, trust is important on eBay, and a verified status means that PayPal effectively testifies that you are who you say you are. It also removes the sending and withdrawal limits on your account (£500 total and £500 per month respectively), which could be important if you buy or sell regularly on eBay. Click the first link.

Become a Verified PayPal Member

Remove Your Sending and Withdrawal Limits.

You can become Verified by setting up Direct Debit and validating your account information. Verification increases the security of the PayPal network and allows you to spend more.

When you become a Verified PayPal member, you're able to:

- Shop without interruption when your Sending Limit is waived
- Withdraw more money from your PayPal account
- Fund payments with your bank account
- Improve your reputation within the PayPal community with the visible status of 'Verified'

In the box below, click on the unticked items to become Verified.

Steps to Verify Your Account	
Set Up Direct Debit	☑
Validate your account information	☐
Supply merchant information	☐

Curiously enough, PayPal offers to call you on the telephone number you provided during registration. You can edit this number now and select, say, your work number instead but you can't use a mobile number. Nor can you use an overseas number. When the call comes, tap in a four-digit number provided by the automated service. Alternatively, you can opt for the postal option and have PayPal send you a letter.

Validate your Account Information by Phone

PayPal needs to confirm that you are located at the address where you receive your credit card statements. To make this confirmation, PayPal will place a quick, automated phone call to the phone number for that address.

Follow the steps below to complete this process.

Step 1: Credit Card Billing Address

Review your credit card information below.

Credit Card: Visa/Delta/Electron XXXX-XXXX-XXXX-0013
Add Credit Card

Billing Address:

United Kingdom
Edit Address

Step 2: Phone Number

Select the phone number **at the address above**, and a time to receive an automated call from PayPal. You must be able to answer the phone at the time you select.

Select Phone: 44- (Home)(Unconfirmed) ▾   Edit Phone   Add Phone

Select Time: ⦿ Call now

⦾ Call in one minute (If you need to disconnect from the Internet first)

You must also complete the merchant information verification process (see the link in Step 21). This involves telling PayPal all about yourself. The form is designed for businesses but you can select Individual in the Type of User field. This done, your account will be 'verified'.

Edit Business Information

We take the privacy of your personal information very seriously. Per our Privacy Policy, please be assured that we will not share your information with outside parties without your knowledge.

Additional Business Information - As this additional information further ensures the security of your account, please make sure that the information you provide is accurate. Some of information below cannot be edited. If you need to change this information, contact PayPal Customer Service. These business details will not be shared with those who purchase from you. Learn more

Type of User: Individual ▾

Date of First Sale: 21 / 08 / 2000
Day Month Year

Account Holder's Date of Birth: 21 / 08 /
Day Month Year

VAT Number: (optional) GB ▾

Category: Computers & Internet ▾

Subcategory: General ▾

Average Transaction Price: Not Applicable ▾

Average Monthly Volume: Not Applicable ▾

Point of Sale: ☑ eBay
☐ Other Marketplace
☐ My Own Website
☐ Other

Your e-commerce URL:

[Save] [Cancel]

PayPal in practice

Let's just round up what we have learned here during the complex PayPal registration procedure. Imagine that you bid £4 for an eBay auction item and win. Postage costs £1 so the seller contacts you with an invoice for £5. You wish to pay through PayPal and the seller has no objection. Both parties have PayPal accounts so the transaction should be very straightforward. Here's what could happen:

● You register a credit card with PayPal and try to make the payment. But the seller has only a Personal PayPal account. This means that he cannot accept a card-funded payment. He must now either refuse your payment and negotiate another form of payment, or upgrade his account to Premier status.

● You take the initiative and say you'll pay the debt by transferring money from your bank account into your PayPal account. This, though, means going through the Direct Debit setup and waiting until PayPal's deposits show up in your bank account. You'll then have to wait again for the slow transfer from bank to PayPal. Unless you already have a Direct Debit mandate in place, it could be weeks before you have cleared funds in your PayPal account.

● Discouraged by having to wait, the seller decides that now is the time to upgrade his account to Premier status. As soon as he completes the procedure, he can claim your £5. That's fine – but at what cost? The seller now has to pay PayPal fees of 3.4% plus 20p. This totals 37p. He ends up with a net balance of £4.63.

From £5 to £4.63 to £4.38 ... and our eBay seller still can't get at his cash.

- Let's now imagine that the seller wants to transfer that £4.63 out of PayPal and into his bank account. This he can do only if he has already completed the tedious Direct Debit procedure described earlier. Failing that, the money is effectively trapped within PayPal.

- With the Direct Debit mandate in place, our seller tries to transfer his £4.63. Only at this point, perhaps, does he appreciate that he'll incur a further charge of 25p. His fiver is now worth a mere £4.38. But he grits his teeth and proceeds.

- Except that he can't! In a final, almost comic, complication, PayPal refuses to let him transfer less than £6 in a single transaction. His money is effectively locked in PayPal until he either earns some more or uses it to fund a PayPal payment.

You don't have to read too closely between the lines to surmise that we are not exactly great fans of PayPal. However, there's simply no getting away from the fact that, for now at least, it is the *de facto* payment method throughout eBay. By all means remain outside the PayPal fold but do so in the full awareness that you'll be unable to bid on many eBay auctions and will certainly reduce your appeal to bidders when it's your turn to sell.

If you do sign up, we suggest that you set up a Premier account, register a credit card for payments (see p148 on fraud prevention for more on why that's important), set up a Direct Debit relationship with your bank so you can transfer money to and from your PayPal account, and verify your account to increase your status. We also recommend that you do all of this right at the outset, not later when you suddenly realise that you've won a PayPal-only auction and need to set up an account, sharpish.

Once you get going with PayPal, managing your money is reasonably straightforward. But getting to this point takes time and patience.

UK Premier Account Overview

Name: Kyle MacRae
Email: _____ (Add email)
Status: UK - Unverified (New)

Balance: £29.15 GBP   View Limits

Recent Activity | All Activity

Your Recent Activity displays the last 7 days of account activity.

File	Type	To/From	Name/Email	Date	Status	Details	Action	Amount	Fee
☐	Transfer	From	Bank Account	21 Oct. 2004	Pending	Details		£25.00 GBP	£0.00 GBP
☐	Payment	To		15 Oct. 2004	Completed	Details		-£5.00 GBP	£0.00 GBP
☐	Transfer	From	Credit Card	15 Oct. 2004	Completed	Details		£5.00 GBP	£0.00 GBP
☐	Transfer	To	Credit Card	15 Oct. 2004	Completed	Details		-£5.00 GBP	£0.00 GBP
☐	Cancelled Payment	From		15 Oct. 2004	Completed	Details		£5.00 GBP	£0.00 GBP
☐	Payment	To		15 Oct. 2004	Cancelled	Details		-£5.00 GBP	£0.00 GBP

4

PART 4 eBay MANUAL

An eBay buyer's guide

PART  Why buy before selling?

Even if you registered with eBay primarily to sell stuff, we suggest that you hold off for a while. eBay is based on trust, and trust is based on feedback. Having a good, ideally perfect feedback profile stands you in better stead for selling because potential bidders can see that other eBayers have had a happy trading experience with you. In fact, many eBayers simply won't buy from somebody with little or zero feedback.

You have to start somewhere, and the easiest way to notch up some positive feedback is by making a few low-cost purchases. Odd though it may seem, you'll get just the same positive feedback score for buying a 50p Dinky model of an Aston Martin as for buying the real thing. It will also prove an invaluable experience, as you'll see the entire eBay trading process from the buyer's perspective – and when you know what's important to a buyer, you'll make a better seller.

We're looking for Betty Blue *on DVD, so we'll start with a simple search on the key phrase* **"betty blue"**. *Note the use of quotation marks to rule out hits for, say, a Betty Bloop doll with blue hair. We're on the hunt for a DVD version of the film so we can narrow the search by adding DVD to the key words or, as here, selecting sellers who categorise their wares correctly. There are seven likely-looking entries in the DVD category.*

From the identical titles, appearance and Buy It Now prices (more of which on p88), we can fairly deduce that four of these items are being sold by the same trader. To verify this, we simply click on each in turn. It happens that the seller has a positive feedback rating of 99.1% with a feedback score of nearly 9000 (i.e. at least 9,000 traders under his belt). PayPal is accepted and there's free postage and packing on offer.

3

This item has been listed with a Buy It Now price of £13.99, which means that we can end the auction early and secure the DVD if we're willing to pay £13.99 right now. This has to be tempting. However, what might the DVD sell for if we waited until the end of the auction? Is £13.00 over the odds?

4

Containing our enthusiasm, we decide to investigate the going rate for Betty Blue DVDs a little further. First, we click the Refine search link and tick the Completed items only box. This will show us any recently completed auctions rather than those that are ongoing.

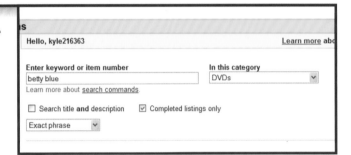

5

As it happens, the seller we looked at in Steps 2 and 3 has sold three copies of Betty Blue recently, all for £13.99. Let's click one of these links to learn a little more.

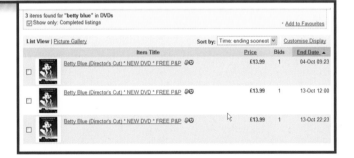

6

We can now see the old auction page for one of the DVDs, complete with the buyer's User ID. If we click this ID , we go to his profile page and can look in the Left for Others section (see Step 6 on p52). Here we can find and read the feedback pertaining to this purchase (assuming that he left feedback).
Alternatively, of course, you can open any seller's profile and browse feedback from buyers.

7

We can broaden the scope of our Betty Blue search by looking for current or past items *available to the UK* rather than *located in the UK* (see p43). In this case, however, it merely throws up one additional copy that was sold from Australia for the equivalent of about £12. Our initial £13.99 with free P&P is looking all the more promising.

8

Just a thought, though. Perhaps we are restricting our search unnecessarily by limiting it to the DVD category only (see Step 1). We repeat the search for **"betty blue"** but this time throw in the keyword **dvd**. We also include items available to the UK (this option is selected from the Refine Search page) to broaden the search further. Surprisingly, perhaps, we now find some 30 listings, several of which did not show up before. One auction is due to end in a little over an hour and is currently priced at only US$6.50.

9

We click that link to find out more. The seller is brand new, has zero feedback, is based in South Korea and wants $7 to ship the DVD. Hmm. We read through the item description carefully.

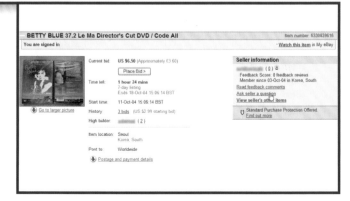

The seller warrants that the DVD is an original copy, not a bootleg, and has included a photograph of what we assume to be the actual item rather than a generic 'stock' photo (see p129 and Appendix 1). However, the disc is described as region-free, which would be extremely unusual for a commercial movie release. But perhaps that's how original movies are marketed in Korea? We decide to ask the seller.

Not a Bootleg DVD or DVD-R

Special Features :
- **Synopsis**
- **Cast & Crew**
- **Director's interview (text)**
- **Awards & Nominations**

Payment Methods

- **PAYPAL** *PayPal* [VISA icons]
- **CASH (U.S. dollar & Euro)**

Shipping Cost

- **$7.00 (Anywhere in the World)** - Add $3.50 for Each Additional DVD

To do this, click the obvious link just below the User ID. This opens an eBay page in which you can compose a freeform question that will go directly to the seller. You don't have direct access to the seller's email address – eBay shields this to protect traders from cranks – but he will receive your message and should respond directly. Be polite, concise and precise.

Ask Seller a Question

Item: BETTY BLUE 37.2 Le Ma Director's Cut DVD / Code All

Enter your question for **sundriverscafe**. eBay will send an email to the seller. S

General question about this item

Hi. I'm curious about whether this DVD is really region-free. Does this mean that I would be able to play it on my Region 2-only player?

Enter up to 1000 characters. HTML cannot be displayed.

☐ Send a copy of this email to myself.
☑ Add this item to my watch list.

Submit question   Cancel

While doing so, note the Add this item to my watch list option. This is one of eBay's most useful features, which we'll come back to shortly. You can also have eBay send you a copy of your own enquiry if you like. A reply duly came confirming the DVD's authenticity. It arrived after the auction closed, mind, but that was our fault for leaving it so late. Then again, if he's really sold 50 copies, why no feedback? We'll return to our quest for this DVD on p92.

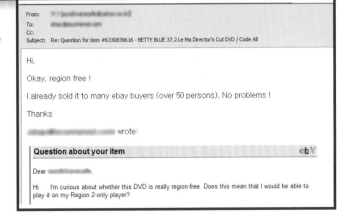

From:
To:
Cc:
Subject: Re: Question for item #6330839616 - BETTY BLUE 37.2 Le Ma Director's Cut DVD / Code All

Hi,

Okay, region free !

I already sold it to many ebay buyers (over 50 persons), No problems !

Thanks

_____ wrote:

Question about your item   ebY

Dear _____,

Hi   I'm curious about whether this DVD is really region-free. Does this mean that I would be able to play it on my Region 2-only player?

Make the most of auction information

An eBay seller has almost unlimited scope to describe an item and you are well advised to read a description in full, especially the payment and postage terms. If you bid on an auction, you are bound by those terms. Here's a roundup of what to look for on an auction page.

Auction details

This section is fully automated by eBay and tells you things you really need to know, such as the current price, the number of bids and, crucially, how long the auction has been running and when it will end. You can also see a summary of postage costs but this is no substitute for reading the terms in detail (see below).

The Add to Calendar link is nowhere near as promising as it sounds. Click this and you'll be prompted to download a VCS file which you can then import into some calendar programs, including Microsoft Outlook. This will, or should, allow you to set a customised reminder that prompts you to log in to eBay and place a bid. But it's a fussy old business, and we hope and suspect that eBay's Calendar will evolve into something more useful.

The key auction information, including the current price, is displayed at the top of the page.

Click the History link to get an idea of the action so far. In this example, there have been 19 bids. What's noteworthy here is that one bidder *appears* to have made several consecutive bids

---

STEIFF - WINNIE THE POOH DISNEY CONVENTION   Item number: 5527337166

You are signed in   · **Watch this item** in My eBay

Current bid:	**£132.00**
	[Place Bid >]
Time left:	**1 day 8 hours**
	10-day listing
	Ends 23-Oct-04 18:37:53 BST
	Add to Calendar
Start time:	13-Oct-04 18:37:53 BST
History:	18 bids (£14.99 starting bid)
High bidder:	(15 ☆)

Item location: London
United Kingdom

Featured Plus! Listing

Post to: Worldwide

Postage costs: £8.00 - Royal Mail Special Delivery

⬇ Go to larger picture

Seller information

(1022 ☆) 🏆 Power Seller

Feedback Score: 1022
Positive Feedback: 100%
Member since 22-Feb-03 in United Kingdom
Read feedback comments
Ask seller a question
View seller's other items
Visit this seller's eBay Shop
Shops

PayPal ✓ Buyer Protection Offered
See coverage and eligibility

User ID	Bid Amount	Date of bid
~~bozella~~ (16 ☆)	£240.00	17-Oct-04 11:12:13 BST
~~sarahamercules~~ (949 ☆) me	£235.00	16-Oct-04 19:22:15 BST
~~nikki~~ (75 ★)	£230.00	16-Oct-04 19:14:06 BST
~~60tunes~~ (1)	£225.00	15-Oct-04 21:29:46 BST
~~sealmon~~ (214 ☆)	£221.00	15-Oct-04 13:56:17 BST
~~60tunes~~ (1)	£210.00	15-Oct-04 21:29:32 BST
~~bozella~~ (16 ☆)	£200.00	15-Oct-04 08:38:07 BST
~~getyonge~~ (45 ☆)	£200.00	15-Oct-04 13:15:32 BST
~~getyonge~~ (45 ☆)	£170.00	15-Oct-04 08:44:43 BST
~~getyonge~~ (45 ☆)	£150.00	15-Oct-04 08:44:33 BST
~~getyonge~~ (45 ☆)	£140.00	15-Oct-04 08:44:19 BST
~~getyonge~~ (45 ☆)	£130.00	15-Oct-04 08:44:09 BST
~~getyonge~~ (45 ☆)	£120.00	15-Oct-04 08:43:57 BST
~~getyonge~~ (45 ☆)	£105.00	14-Oct-04 13:16:16 BST
~~ita625~~ (29 ☆)	£85.00	14-Oct-04 21:38:16 BST
~~mascindi~~ (272 ☆)	£78.00	14-Oct-04 04:36:36 BST
~~sixhead~~ (98 ★)	£50.50	14-Oct-04 07:42:08 BST
~~Ikaul~~ (112 ☆)	£26.01	14-Oct-04 07:27:48 BST
~~sronagu~~ (271 ☆)	£23.09	14-Oct-04 03:59:19 BST

very close together. Why does he keep outbidding himself, you might wonder? But this is illusory. What's really happening here is that somebody else has been trying to reach and breach his hidden proxy bid. Eventually, at £200, he is beaten, as evidenced by the two identical bids of £200 (see p14-17 for a similar example).

View a seller's other items

When a user has more than one auction in progress, eBay adds a View seller's other items link to each auction page. This can be fruitful indeed. You may find, for instance, that somebody selling a child's toy also has some children's books and a car safety seat for sale elsewhere. It's obviously hit and miss but there's every chance that you'll find a degree of shared tastes between you.

Seller information

(3)
Feedback Score: 3
Positive Feedback: 100%
Member since 07-Sep-04 in United Kingdom
Read feedback comments
Ask seller a question
View seller's other items

🛡 Standard Purchase Protection Offered.
Find out more

Postage and payment details

Postage Cost	Services Available	Available to
£9.50	Other Courier	United Kingdom Only
£15.00	Other courier or delivery service	Europe
£25.00	Other courier or delivery service	Americas, Australia

Will post to Worldwide

Postage insurance
Included in postage and packing cost

Seller's payment instructions and return policy
I can accept all online payments plus cheques, postal orders, cash (by insured delivery). I can only accept credit cards when used in conjunction with an online payment company (like paypal or fastpay) Please note that I do not charge a penny to buyers wanting to use online payment houses or any other form of payment.

Payment and postage

To skip straight to an auction's postage and payment terms, click the handy hyperlink positioned just below the item.

If you read here that postage charges will be calculated only after the auction, don't bid. It is the seller's responsibility to tell you how much you'll have to pay. If in any doubt at all, ask the seller for clarification. And if you don't get it, walk away.

In particular, establish exactly how an international package will be delivered: by air mail, by surface mail or by courier? How long should delivery take? Can you opt for a speedier method if you're prepared to pay for the privilege or does the seller tie you to one option? Will you be hit with import, clearance or duty charges at customs when the item arrives in the UK? If the seller has few feedback points, ask whether he has experience of shipping overseas and knows what paperwork is required. Also check his profile feedback for comments from UK-based customers. Be wary if you come across the likes of: 'Delighted with the item when it arrived ... eventually. Shame about the Customs bill!'

If postal insurance is offered, this means that the seller is prepared to insure the item against non-delivery. You may be expected to meet the additional cost. It's an attractive option for valuable items when you consider the impasse that can arise when a seller says that he shipped an item but it fails to show up and you end up out of pocket. If the package was insured the seller should be able to make a claim and reimburse you. Then again, most packages arrive safely and the norm on eBay is not to insure items in transit. By all means ask a seller if they will consider insurance if the prospect of losing a package in the post alarms you. However, if you wait until the auction has ended, don't be surprised if the seller politely points out that it was clear from the auction terms that insurance was part of the deal.

Pay very close attention indeed to payment terms. Here, the seller 'prefers' PayPal but no other acceptable forms of payment are listed. At the very least, this would warrant sending a question to the seller ('Do you also take cheques?', for example).

Credit and debit cards are listed but this is rather misleading. If you look closely, you'll see that these are in parentheses after the PayPal logo. All this means is that the seller has a Premier (or Business) PayPal account, which means he can take card-funded payments from another PayPal account. On the face of it, you would think that the seller takes credit cards directly, but that's not the case.

It's essential to factor in the cost of postage and insurance before bidding.

Payment methods accepted

This seller, ▓▓▓▓ ▓▓▓▓, prefers PayPal.

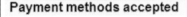

- Personal cheque
- Postal Order or Banker's Draft
- Other - See Payment Instructions for payment methods accepted

Learn about payment methods.

PayPal preferred – a common sight on eBay.

Item descriptions

Some auction items are described in a couple of words and others with pages of text and multiple photos. The approach depends more on a given seller's inclinations and effort than on the properties of the item itself. It's common to find a 7" vinyl single that's worth perhaps £1.50 more carefully described than jewellery worth a hundred times as much. There are no rules, and you must simply take an item as you find it or press the seller for further relevant information. In all innocence, a seller may forget to include a vital specification or detail in an original description.

Most eBay auctions are enhanced with product photographs. In these days of digital cameras, many sellers have the wherewithal to take a snapshot or two of their item. Others prefer to use a 'stock' photograph of the product rather than the actual item that's for sale. Such photos are often pinched from websites like Amazon or a manufacturer's or retailer's online catalogue. Use your own judgment here. If you're buying a new, sealed CD or DVD, a photograph of the actual item that you stand to win adds nothing of value to the equation. But if you're in the market for a second-hand car, you aren't going to settle for a scanned image from an old, oil-stained Haynes manual ('It looks just like this, only three years older, and without the alloys or sunroof, and a bit scratched around the wings. And it's blue.').

Check exactly what you're buying before you make a bid.

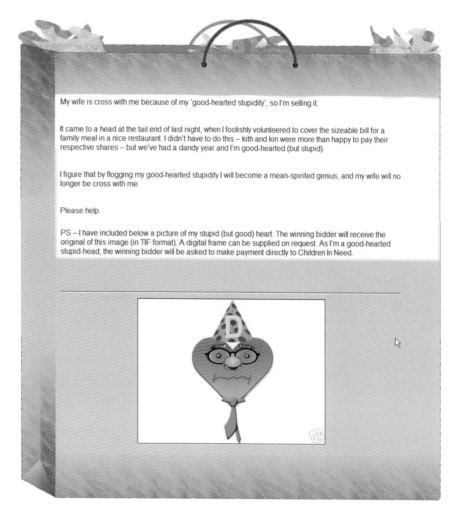

My wife is cross with me because of my 'good-hearted stupidity', so I'm selling it.

It came to a head at the tail end of last night, when I foolishly volunteered to cover the sizeable bill for a family meal in a nice restaurant. I didn't have to do this – kith and kin were more than happy to pay their respective shares – but we've had a dandy year and I'm good-hearted (but stupid).

I figure that by flogging my good-hearted stupidity I will become a mean-spirited genius, and my wife will no longer be cross with me.

Please help.

PS – I have included below a picture of my stupid (but good) heart. The winning bidder will receive the original of this image (in TIF format). A digital frame can be supplied on request. As I'm a good-hearted stupid-head, the winning bidder will be asked to make payment directly to Children In Need.

Asking questions

As already mentioned, ask the seller if there is anything at all that concerns you about the terms of an auction or the item itself. We really can't stress this strongly enough. Sellers expect to be queried and have a duty to respond quickly and accurately. eBay only works at all because users engage in this level of interaction, and the use of negative feedback is all too often a sign that buyer or seller or both failed to communicate properly when communication would have helped. Never be reluctant to ask a seller a question, and be very cautious indeed about bidding when you don't like – or especially if you don't receive – a reply.

One thing to note is that when you send a seller a question, you do so through the eBay web form, as seen in Step 11 on p75. But when the seller replies, he does so directly, which means you'll get to see his actual email address. Obviously this opens up all manner of possibilities for behind-the-scenes private dealing.

There's nothing in the world to stop a real or potential bidder and seller from striking up a relationship. For instance, you may be prepared to bid on an incomplete series of Churchill's Diaries and the seller, a book dealer, promises to look out for the missing volume and sell it to you directly at cost price in the future rather than listing it at auction. Just bear in mind that eBay won't have anything to do with such a private arrangement: if the deal goes bad, you're on your own. Some people will say anything to make a sale, so be seriously sceptical and use your discretion. If somebody makes an outright offer to deal directly on an item already in an auction, you can be sure that they're just trying to avoid paying eBay's fees. Walk away.

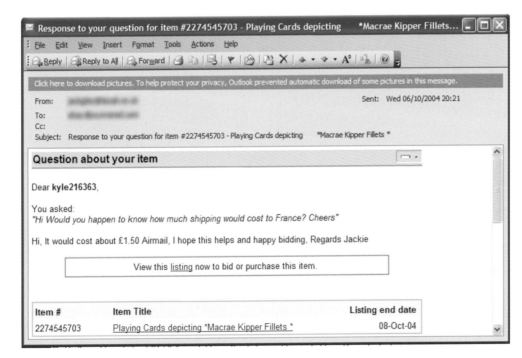

Don't be shy – ask a seller a question. Email exchanges are expected on eBay and can help clarify item or shipping information.

Currency and language

With international trading, the seller dictates which currency he will accept and the buyer must abide. If you see an item priced in Euros, then expect to pay in Euros. PayPal UK lets you pay somebody in Sterling, US or Canadian dollars, Euros or Yen. With any other currency, you'll have to come to an arrangement with the seller. For instance, they may accept US dollars but insist upon a small surcharge. PayPal performs currency conversions automatically at a cost of 2.5% above its bank's wholesale rate. eBay itself also has a currency converter at **http://pages.ebay.co.uk/services/buyandsell/ currencyconverter.htm**l.

You may come across eBay auctions in foreign languages, particularly if you search for items available to the UK rather than just those sold within the UK. You may find that the seller provides a bi- or multilingual listing but, if not, you really don't have the right to ask for a translation (any more than you would expect to have to translate one of your own auctions into Japanese). To get the gist, run the page or text through one of the online automatic translation services like AltaVista's Babel Fish at **http://world.altavista.com**. If there's anything that remains unclear, feel free to ask the seller a question, but have the courtesy to do so in his own language. Again, an online translation tool can help you construct a basic question.

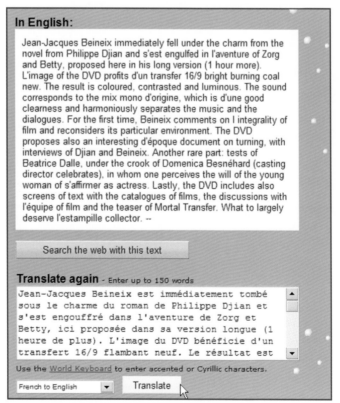

When language is a barrier, online tools like Babel Fish can be helpful (to a degree).

Shadow another bidder

We've already shown how to view a seller's other items but how about finding out what other bidders are interested in? Think of this as an alternative, almost radical way to browse eBay. On the assumption that anybody bidding on an item that interests you must, to a degree at least, have similar tastes, you can potentially use their bid history to uncover other items of interest and perhaps also find valuable traders who specialise in relevant fields. Here's how.

1

Let's say that there are a number of bids on a widescreen TV. On the bid history page (see p76-77), you can view each bidder's User ID. Look for an eBayer with a good positive feedback rating and lots of trades, and click his ID. This takes you to his profile page.

●●●● (1)	£125.00	21-Oct-04 21:44:49 BST
●●●●●● (1) ⑧	£120.00	21-Oct-04 21:16:17 BST
●●●● (1)	£120.00	21-Oct-04 21:44:36 BST
●●●● (1)	£115.00	21-Oct-04 21:44:23 BST
●●●●●●●● (0) ⑧	£110.49	21-Oct-04 21:15:40 BST
●●●●●● (1) ⑧	£105.00	21-Oct-04 21:15:30 BST
●●●●●●●●●●● (2)	£103.00	21-Oct-04 18:55:46 BST
●●●●●●● (5)	£97.49	21-Oct-04 20:59:19 BST
●●●●●●● (5)	£91.49	21-Oct-04 20:59:01 BST
●●●●●●●● (3) ⑧	£75.00	21-Oct-04 15:54:54 BST
●●●● (43 ☆)	£50.00	21-Oct-04 16:45:35 BST
●●●● (7)	£31.00	21-Oct-04 15:37:00 BST
●●●●●● (126 ☆)	£20.00	21-Oct-04 14:55:16 BST
●●●● (7)	£20.00	21-Oct-04 15:36:41 BST

2

Open the From Sellers tab to access feedback left by sellers, and click on any item code to discover what your target bought recently – and how much he paid. Although it feels like snooping, this is perfectly legitimate behaviour on eBay.

All Feedback Received	From Buyers	From Sellers	Left for Others

9 feedback received by m7mario from sellers (0 mutually withdrawn)

Comment	From
⊕ Prompt Payment. No Hassles. Excellent Buyer. A+++!	Seller
⊕ Great ebayer!!! A++++	Seller 1287 ⇗
⊕ VERY FAST PAYMENT. HIGHLY RECOMMENDED.THANKS FOR THE DEAL.	Seller
⊕ This buyer made ebay the most comfortable place to sell things!	Seller no long
⊕ ++++Superb Buyer... Best of the Best in Ebay... Thank you! AAAA++++	Seller

3

But there's a better way to spy upon – sorry, to 'shadow' – another eBayer. Back in the bid history page, make a note of your target's User ID. Now hold down the shift key on your keyboard (the key that turns capital letters on and off) and click the Advanced Search link near the Search button. A new search page will open in a separate browser window.

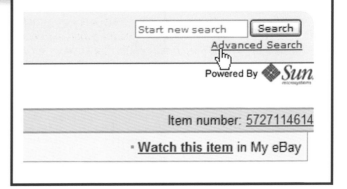

In the sidebar on the Advanced Search page, click *Items by Bidder*. Now enter the User ID that you noted in Step 3. Check the box that expands the search to include completed listings and click Search.

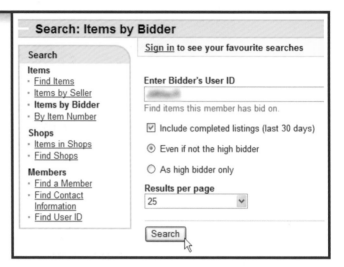

You now have a very useful summary of items that this user has bid on in the recent past or is bidding on now, replete with descriptions and clickable links. You might, for instance, discover that he is currently involved in an auction for a cheaper widescreen TV. Perhaps you didn't spot that item during your search for a widescreen TV and you'll now bid against your shadow for that item.

You can also glean valuable information about traders from this page. For instance, your target may have lost an earlier auction for a widescreen TV. If you now click that seller's ID, you may well find that he has a similar or identical TV for sale right now.

When you find a trader that interests you, even if only for future reference, click the Add to Favourite Sellers link. You can now keep tabs on this seller from your My eBay page. Repeat as often as you like. 'Shadowing' is a slow process with many dead ends but we assure you that it can prove fruitful.

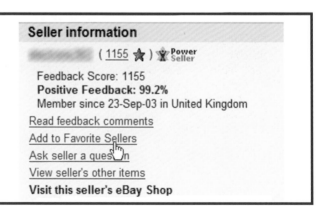

PART **The eBay watch list**

eBay has several tools to help you keep track of auctions
in progress but by far the most useful is the My eBay
watch list. Here's how it works.

Search or browse for any item that you might want to
bid for. Today, we rather fancy a Hornby locomotive. In
the Time Left area, we can see that this auction was set
to run for seven days and is now very near to closing.
We don't want to bid just yet – see the bidding
strategies (p90-91) for the reasons why – but nor do
we want to forget about it.

Click the Watch this item link. The web page doesn't
change at this point but something interesting happens
behind the scenes. Now find a couple of similar items
to monitor and click Watch this item for each. When
you're finished, click the My eBay button at the top of
the page.

We saw the My eBay sidebar earlier when we saved a
search but look now for the All Buying and Start Selling
links. These lead to details of auctions that you're
currently involved in, if any. As of yet, we haven't placed
any bids and we're not selling anything. However, we
have added three auctions to our watch list. This can
be accessed via the Watching link under All Buying.

Here you have an extremely useful summary of auctions you want to keep tabs on. At a glance, you can see the current price, the number of bids, the auction closing time and a reminder of the seller's ID and rating.

To go straight to an auction, click the item title. To remove an item, put a check in the box next to the title and click the Delete button. To add new items, repeat steps 1 and 2. You can have up to 100 items listed here at any one time. To be sure that you're always seeing the most up to date information, use the Refresh link (or your web browser's refresh button).

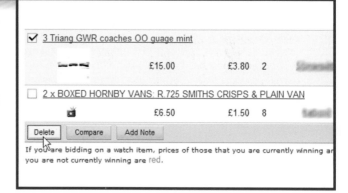

When an auction in your watch list closes, it moves to a separate Ended page. This is useful for keeping track of prices. For instance, you might want to monitor a dozen Hornby locomotive auctions to get an accurate feel for the market value before placing a bid yourself. Clear out old items when you're through with them.

As you use eBay more and more, you might want to use the Customise Summary link on the My eBay page to add extra information to the page. For instance, you can view your saved searches and feedback record all on the one page.

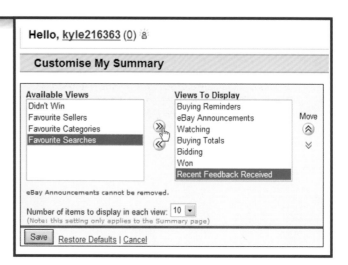

You can add notes to items in your watch list, which is a handy way of reminding yourself why you want to bid for this item and how high you are prepared to go. You could also use notes to store a seller's response if you ask a question. Put a check in the box next to the item in question and click Add Note. Enter a message (for some reason the note tool can't handle apostrophes) and click Save. Your note is now appended to the item in your watch list. Use the Edit link if you want to make a change.

When your watch list grows to unmanageable dimensions, as seems to be the norm on eBay, use the different headings to re-sort items in a number of ways. By default, items are listed in order of auction closing time – soonest first – but you can just as easily view items by current price. This is handy if you are watching several auctions with the same item and hope to grab the best bargain.

eBay will also send you email reminders whenever an item on your watch list is drawing to a close. This is particularly useful when you add a must-have item to your watch list and then forget all about it for a week or more.

Finally, don't neglect eBay customer announcements. These appear frequently in My eBay and often herald an important shift in the User Agreement or warn of an impending downtime in the service. As an eBay user, you owe it to yourself to keep abreast of the service, especially when that service is in a constant state of flux (ditto PayPal).

PART 4

Understanding auction prices

At any given time, each eBay auction has a price, but it's important to understand just how that price comes about. There are several possibilities:

Starting price Every item listed on eBay has a starting price, akin to an auctioneer asking: 'Now who'll start me at £100?' It's entirely possible to win an auction by bidding the starting price but only if nobody else bids higher. If nobody bids at all, the auction will close without a sale.

No bids yet but the starting price is a cool £1,125.

Starting bid	**£1,125.00**
	Place Bid >
Time left:	**9 hours 56 mins**
	1-day listing
	Ends 01-Dec-04 20:15:45 GMT
Start time:	30-Nov-04 20:15:45 GMT
History:	0 bids
Item location:	POWYS
	United Kingdom

Highest bid This is either equal to or higher than the starting bid. The highest bidder at the close of an auction wins the item. Unless ...

With 17 bids in the bag, the current auction leader stands to snaffle a bargain.

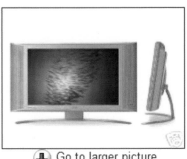

Current bid:	**£295.00**
	Place Bid >
Time left:	**9 hours 31 mins**
	1-day listing
	Ends 01-Dec-04 19:52:17 GMT
Start time:	30-Nov-04 19:52:17 GMT
History:	17 bids (£1.00 starting bid)
High bidder:	▓▓▓▓ (0)

Reserve price As in a live auction, a seller can set a reserve price. This is the price below which he is not prepared to – and cannot be compelled to – sell. The trouble is, bidders have no way of knowing what the reserve price is. On a digital camera with a starting price, the reserve price might be £27 or £100. There is no binding relationship between the starting price and the reserve price, and choosing the right prices is one of the trickiest aspects of listing an item on eBay (as we shall see). For now, we will simply point out three factors.

● When you place a bid on an item with a reserve price, eBay tells you (and the rest of the world) instantly whether or not the reserve price has been met. This way, you always know that you're competing against a hidden reserve price even if you don't know what it is.

● Setting a reserve price for an auction item is entirely optional and one that can discourage potential bidders.

● If you explicitly state in your item description that an item is being sold *without* a reserve, this is immediately attractive to bidders as it suggest the possibility of a bargain. Unless a seller sets a reserve, he must sell to the highest bidder – even if there is only one bidder and even if he bids only the starting price.

When the reserve price has not been met, it begs the question of how high you would have to go to stand even a chance of winning the item.

Current bid:	**£180.00 (Reserve not met)**
	[Place Bid >]
Time left:	**3 hours 22 mins**
	5-day listing
	Ends 01-Dec-04 13:39:44 GMT
Start time:	26-Nov-04 13:39:44 GMT
History:	9 bids (£1.00 starting bid)
High bidder:	(2)

Go to larger picture

Buy It Now When you see a Buy It Now icon next to an auction item, you know that you can secure that item instantly by paying the asking price. This was the case with our search for a Betty Blue DVD earlier (see the screenshots on p72). If a digital camera was listed with a Buy It Now price of £50, we could pay £50 immediately to 'win' the item and end the auction.

However, there are three quirks to the system (as always on eBay).

● The Buy It Now option disappears the moment somebody places a bid below the Buy It Now price. Let's suppose that a camera has a starting price of £25, no reserve, and a Buy It Now price of £50. If a bidder comes along and bids £25, the Buy It Now price vanishes and the camera must now be sold in open auction. Nobody can now pay £50 to end the auction early.

● The second quirk is an exception to that rule. Where an auction attracts a bid but that bid is lower than the reserve price, the Buy It Now icon stays in place. Thus it's possible to find an auction with active bids and a Buy It Now price. The Buy It Now price only disappears when the reserve price has been met.

● The third thing is that some auctions only have a Buy It Now price. That is, the only way to get the item is buy paying the Buy It Now price. The price is effectively fixed and bids are not accepted. Clearly, a Buy It Now auction is not an auction at all but a fixed price sale. Many buyers prefer Buy It Now auctions because it removes the hassle, uncertainty and delay associated with eBay auctions.

You can easily sniff out Buy It Now auctions or sales on eBay. From any search results page, click the Buy It Now tab to see only those with a Buy It Now price. Alternatively, use the Advanced Search page at the outset to exclude items that do not have a Buy It Now price; or click the Refine Search link to narrow your hits at any subsequent point.

The current price of any item in any eBay auction is thus an amalgam of several possibilities:

Starting price (minimum opening bid)

Reserve price (an optional, hidden minimum selling price)

Current high bid (the highest bid so far, which may or may not meet the reserve)

Buy It Now (an optional, public price that ends the auction immediately)

But there's a further, all-important issue to consider …

Proxy bidding revisited

In an eBay auction, you can either bid the minimum increment, which is fixed on a sliding scale, or place a proxy bid. A proxy bid is the highest price that you are prepared to pay but it remains hidden from other bidders unless and until it is breached. See the example on p14-17 for a refresher.

This means that the current auction price is not *necessarily* the highest bid. As a simple example, a CD might have attracted one bid of £5. The minimum bid increment is 50p so you bid £5.50. But the current auction price instantly jumps to £6. You have been outbid by proxy.

You should certainly consider placing a proxy bid yourself. Let's say that you are prepared to pay £10 for the CD that currently stands at £5. All you have to do is place a £10 bid. There's no special process, for *all eBay bids are proxies by default*. If there are no other proxy bids in place, the CD price moves to £5.50 in your favour. If there is already a proxy bid in place but your bid is higher, the CD price goes to the value of the first proxy plus the required bid increment.

Let's follow this a little further. If you bid £10 for the CD and there are no earlier proxies, you stand to win it for £5.50. But say somebody comes along and bids £6.00. The eBay system will automatically raise your bid to £6.50. If the other bidder raises the stakes to £7, eBay ups your bid to £7.50. And so on all the way up to £10. Only when somebody bids higher than your proxy can you lose.

But then, *you would have lost anyway* if £10 really is your top price.

From proxy to snipe

Proxy bidding may seem unnatural – indeed, it is unnatural in an auction environment – but that's the eBay way. The easiest way to win any auction is by placing one bid that reflects your true maximum. You may win the auction for significantly less, or you may be outbid, but you will never be caught up in a last-minute bidding war and potentially provoked into bidding way over the odds. At the very least, it saves you the hassle of keeping tabs on the auction and returning time and time again to up your bids.

It's also true that the presence of a hidden proxy puts many bidders off. After bidding £5.50 and seeing the price jump to £6 in somebody else's favour, would you bid a second time or would you walk away and look elsewhere? If you do decide to bid on, why bother inching towards the hidden proxy in the hope of stealing the lead by a penny or two? It's so much easier just to bid your true maximum on a one-off bid. If it breaches the prior proxy, fantastic: you'll lead the auction and the onus to overtake you is elsewhere. If not ... well, you didn't want to pay more than that anyway so where's the harm? You've saved yourself a good deal of time and can look for an alternative item at a price that's right.

It also has the advantage of potentially beating a late 'snipe' bid (much more of which on pp101-113). For instance, an auction could sit at £5.50 for ages, backed by your hidden £10 proxy. In the final seconds, somebody places a £9.50 bid. There's no time left to up your own bid but you don't need to: your £10 beats the sniper's £9.50, and you win. Of course, if the snipe was higher than £10, you would lose – but then *you would have lost anyway*. Again, the notion of a true maximum – the price that you will go to but not under any circumstances beyond – is critical.

You can't bid less than the minimum bid increment but you can certainly bid higher.

A hidden proxy bid will beat other bidders automatically, but that's not always a good thing.

For all that, proxy bidding is not without its flaws. For one thing, placing a proxy bid early on in an auction means showing your hand, at least to the extent of revealing your interest in the item. It can be better to lay low and make a high proxy bid right at the end of the auction. This is the basis of sniping.

Similarly, a bidder may be frustrated if his first bid is beaten by a proxy and will determinedly bang away at it, increment by increment. An early proxy bid can fuel a one-sided bidding war and drive the auction price close to or beyond your true maximum. Again, the answer is to place a proxy bid late in the auction.

Snipe smart ...

Sniping is when you place a bid *very* late in the day, ideally within the final seconds. You can either bid the minimum increment, in which case you risk being beaten by a hidden proxy; or place a proxy yourself, in which case you can only be beaten by an even higher proxy. Like it or loathe it, sniping is increasingly the strategy of choice on eBay.

Consider these scenarios:

● A CD sits at £5.50 as the auction draws to a close. With a minute to go, you make a bid of £6. Oops, it's not enough. The earlier bidder's hidden proxy trumps your bid and takes

When you have an auction in your sights, snipe it at the last possible moment.

the CD to £6.50, entirely automatically. You want to bid higher, all the way to £10 if need be ... but time is up. Unfortunately, you had no way of knowing in advance that the current £5.50 bid was backed by a proxy.

● With an hour to go, the CD is priced at £5.50. You judge that now is the time to place a high proxy bid, so you bid your true maximum, £10. You immediately take the lead at £6, which tells you that there are no other proxies at play. To be beaten now, somebody has to bid higher than £10. Chances are that the CD will attract a couple of last-minute bids but you have every chance of winning. Still, there's time enough left for somebody to overtake your proxy and beat you with a bid of £10.50.

● The CD is currently priced at any level below your true maximum. With five seconds left on the auction clock, you bid £10. This is a classic snipe. No other bidders have time to see your bid, let alone work out what your proxy is and beat it by a few pence. The only way you can be beaten is if somebody else bids higher than £10 at the same time.

It boils down to this: if you bid your true maximum in a last-second snipe, you will definitely win the auction *if the auction is winnable at that price*. If you don't win, it is because somebody is prepared to pay more than you. It really is as simple as that.

... don't snipe silly

Of course, it stands to reason that you can win any auction by placing an extremely high snipe. On the CD, for instance, you might bid £50 just in case there's a hidden proxy of, say, £10.01. If you were only to bid £10, you would lose for the sake of a penny (which is classic post-auction rationalisation: 'If only I had gone the extra penny/pound!'). Your £50 snipe would win you the CD at a price of £10.51.

But we trust you can spot the two flaws with this approach.

● Somebody else may have the same idea and place, say, a £45 snipe a second or two before you place your snipe. This is a very real and growing danger on eBay. It means that you could end up paying £46 for a CD worth £10.

● An inflated silly snipe completely demolishes the notion of your true maximum bid. That's just crazy. Regardless of how you choose to bid on eBay, *you must decide in advance exactly how much you are prepared to pay*. Do not wait to see how high the item goes and risk getting swept along in the excitement of a last-minute bidding war.

In fact, we'll go further and suggest that if you place a proxy bid that reflects your *true maximum*, you shouldn't monitor an auction at all. What would be the point? If you get outbid, you get outbid, and that's just too bad. If getting outbid makes you change your mind and raise your bid, then you clearly didn't know what your true maximum was earlier. That is a dangerous game to play and no way at all to win at eBay.

See p101 for more on sniping.

PART 4 'Winning' a Buy It Now auction

There's no secret or trick to winning a Buy It Now eBay auction; all you have to do is pay the fixed price and the deal is done. Here's how.

1

Login to your eBay account and search for an item. If you're more concerned with practice and feedback than anything else, look for something cheap. We'll return to our Betty Blue DVD from earlier. There are still copies available for £13.99 on a Buy It Now basis, with free postage.

2

As always, read the seller's feedback and check the terms of the auction. In this case, the seller makes it crystal clear that he expects both immediate payment and payment via PayPal only. That's fine, because our PayPal account is up and running. Very simply, I click the Buy It Now button next to the price.

3

One of eBay's most irritating traits is forcing you to sign in again with your password even when you are already logged in. This is particularly infuriating when you're trying to place a last-minute bid on an auction that's closing, as you can easily miss the end.

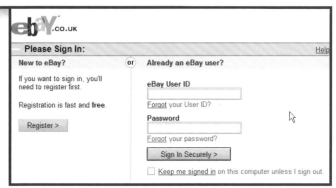

4 Another reminder here that the seller wants immediate payment. Having checked that the delivery address is correct and that I agree with the amount – £13.99 and no postage – I can click the Continue to PayPal button. This delivery address is about to become important. In eBay, you can set up two addresses: one where the account is registered, which will usually be your home address; and a separate delivery address (see Step 4 on p31). You might, for instance, use a business address for deliveries because somebody will always be there to receive parcels. I chose my business address here.

5 You'll be prompted to log in to your PayPal account now. Check the details on the payment page very carefully indeed. For instance, you may need to amend the postage costs if you're asking for the item to be shipped overseas.

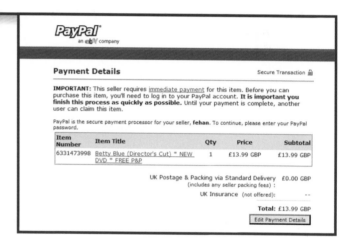

6 Choose your payment poison. By default, PayPal is configured to make payments via direct debit from my bank account. This is 'backed up' by the credit card I registered, which means PayPal will take the payment from my card should my bank refuse the cash transfer. If I had cleared funds in my PayPal account, I could use those instead.

7 I actually want to pay by credit card because that provides me with additional protection in the event of a bad deal (see p148). In extremis, such as non-delivery, I could ask my credit card provider to 'chargeback' the £13.99 to PayPal, which would then have to try to recover the money from the seller's account (something that PayPal is none too keen on). I click the More Funding Options link to access my PayPal preferences and make the change.

The next screen tries to persuade me to pay from my bank account instead. PayPal informs me that the purchase is eligible for £250 of Buyer Protection (see p149), presumably with the implication that I don't need the added security of credit card protection.

Funding Confirmation   Secure Transaction 🔒

Before deciding to fund your payment with a debit or credit card, consider the benefits of paying with your bank account:

- **This payment is eligible for up to <u>£250.00 GBP</u> of coverage with 🛡 <u>PayPal Buyer Protection</u>.**
- Paying with your bank account is instant and your payment will be completed immediately — just as easy as paying with cash
- PayPal keeps your bank account information safe and secure through military-grade encryption and 100% coverage of any unauthorised use
- Easy - use the same bank account for making payments and withdrawals

Do you still want to change your funding source to a credit card?

[Yes]   [No]

Suddenly, the system breaks down. PayPal ask me to confirm my delivery address but it shows my home address, not the delivery address I specified in eBay in Step 4. There is an Edit Address button on the PayPal page but this simply leads back to eBay where my business address is correctly listed. When I return to PayPal, my home address appears again. There seems to be no way to change this.

Delivery Information

Postal Address:

United Kingdom
Confirmed ❓
[Edit Address]

Not knowing whether the seller will receive instructions to send the DVD to my home address or to my delivery address, I decide to add a note for clarification. The PayPal form has a box for just such a purpose. This will hopefully avoid confusion. We shall see. All that remains is to click the Pay button.

Message to Seller (Optional)

I'm not sure which delivery address you'll see
when this order comes through -- eBay and paypal
can't seem to co-ordinate -- but I'd like to
confirm that it should be:

[Pay]   [Cancel]

And that's that. PayPal draws £13.99 from my credit card account and pays the same to the seller. I also receive a near-instant email that confirms the payment and, as I feared, shows the wrong delivery address. However, the email does give me the seller's direct email address so I can contact him directly for clarification.

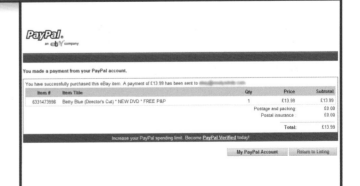

Back on eBay, the auction page confirms the deal. There is a link to check the status of my payment and, wouldn't you know it, the seller has been instructed to ship to my home address. Just to be clear here: eBay knew where I wanted the DVD to go and stated my business address correctly but PayPal instructed the seller to ship it to my home address and this overrode My eBay preference. As a glitch, it's infuriating. See Step 14 for the resolution.

On the My eBay page, there are a couple of welcome changes. The Won link in the All Buying section of the sidebar now has a (1) after it – I can click this to view the transaction details – and there's a prompt to leave feedback. However, I would be very unwise to do so until I have received the DVD. When and whether I will receive the DVD has been rather complicated by the earlier confusion. Let's try to sort that out now ...

I go rooting around in PayPal and access my Profile page. There, under Account Information, is a Postal Address link. By clicking this, I discover that I can add up to 29 different addresses. In a sense, this is handy. I can now add my business address and select it as the delivery address next time I conduct a PayPal transaction. But the fact remains that I couldn't specify the correct delivery address at the time of placing the order because PayPal overrode My eBay preference.

One final rant on this subject. It so happens that I wanted to send the DVD to a friend overseas as a gift but PayPal does not let you add non-UK delivery addresses. The upshot is that you have to take separate measures to make a seller aware of your wishes (always assuming that they are prepared to ship abroad in the first place, of course).

PART  # Placing incremental and proxy bids

This time around, I'll behave like most newcomers to eBay and bid the minimum increment on an auction item. This is what you would do at a live auction, after all, and it feels very natural. It is not, however, the way to win on eBay. Here's why.

Here's a brand new bilingual dictionary on CD, currently priced at £2.20 but worth £30 in the shops. The auction has three of its ten days left to run and has already attracted four low bids. I decide that I'll pay up to £10 (plus the postage). The obvious Place Bid button invites a click.

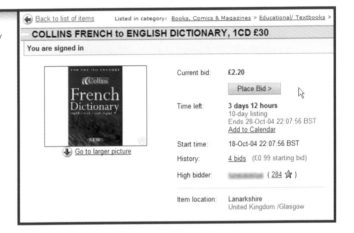

The bid increment for an item priced between £1.01 and £5 is 20p, so eBay tells me that I have to bid at least £2.40. I enter this amount and click Continue.

Place a Bid

Hello kyle216363! (Not you?) Enter your maximum bid and click **Continue**.

Item title:	COLLINS FRENCH to ENGLISH DICTIONARY, 1CD £30
Current bid:	£2.20
Your maximum bid:	£ 2.40 (Enter £2.40 **or more**)

Continue >   You will confirm in the next step.

eBay automatically bids on your behalf **up to** your maximum bid. Learn about bidding.

This is the last chance to back out. I review the terms carefully and note the £1 for postal insurance. I hadn't noticed this before, so it's worth further investigation. Using the web browser's Back button, I retreat a couple of steps to return to the item page.

Review and Confirm Bid

Hello kyle216363! (Not you?)

Item title:	COLLINS FRENCH to ENGLISH DICTIONARY, 1CD £30
Your maximum bid:	**£2.40**
Postage and packing:	£1.50 - Seller's Standard Rate (within United Kingdom).
Postal insurance:	£1.00
Payment methods:	PayPal, Personal cheque, Postal Order or Banker's Draft, Other - See Payment Instructions.

By clicking on the button below, you commit to buy this item from the seller if you're the winning bidder.

Confirm Bid

You are agreeing to a contract -- You will enter into a legally binding contract to purchase the item from the seller if you're responsible for reading the full item listing, including the seller's instructions and accepted payment methods. Seller assumes item.

4

It transpires that the insurance is an optional extra so I should be given the chance to choose whether or not I want it later – but only, of course, if I win the auction. I can now return to Step 3 with my browser's Forward button (or via the Place Bid button on the item's eBay page).

Postage and payment details

Postage Cost	Services Available	Available to
£1.50	Seller's Standard Rate	United Kingdom Only

Will post to Worldwide

Postage insurance
£1.00 Optional

Escrow
Available.

5

This time, I click Confirm Bid. eBay takes a moment or two to process my bid… and then tells me that I've been outbid! The CD now stands at £2.60. At this point, many (all?) newcomers to eBay scratch their heads in puzzlement and despair. How is this possible? The answer, of course, is that somebody else has placed a higher proxy bid. How high, I don't know – and the only way to find out is to raise my bid until I breach it.

Bid Confirmation   Item number: 6932939518

Hello kyle216363! (Not you?)   This item is being tracked in My eBay

✗ You've been outbid. Bid again for another chance to win this item.

Important: Another bidder placed a higher maximum bid than yours, possibly **days or hours before**. To increase your chances of winning, enter the **highest** amount you would be willing to pay below.

Title: COLLINS FRENCH to ENGLISH DICTIONARY, 1CD £30
Time left: 3 days 12 hours
History: 5 bids
Current bid: £2.60
Your new maximum bid: £ [   ] (Enter £2.80 **or more**)

[Bid Again >]

How did this happen? eBay compares your bid to those of others. You were outbid because another bidder placed a higher maximum bid.

How does bidding work? eBay automatically bids on your behalf **up to** your maximum bid. If the item ends for less than your maximum, that's all you'll have to pay. See example.

Reminder: Even if you don't bid again, you could still end up as the winning bidder if higher bids are retracted or canceled. Continue to check the status of this item until it ends.

6

Three options. First, I can bid the minimum increment of 20p and see what happens. If I am still outbid, I can bid again, and again. Secondly, I can immediately bid my true maximum of £10. This will either better the previous proxy (or proxies), in which case I'll lead the auction, or it won't, in which case I should walk away now. Or thirdly, I can wait. I take the first approach.

Title: COLLINS FRENCH to ENGLISH DICTIONARY, 1CD £30
Time left: 3 days 12 hours
History: 5 bids
Current bid: £2.60
Your new maximum bid: £ [2.80] (Enter £2.80 **or more**)

[Bid Again >]

Ho hum. £2.80 just isn't going to beat the hidden proxy. So I skip to strategy two and bid my true maximum of £10. Be very sure to use decimal points when entering large amounts; miss it here, and I could end up bidding £1,000. Will £10 be enough?

Bid Confirmation

Hello kyle216363! (Not you?)

✗ **You've been outbid. Bid again for another chance to win this item.**

Want to increase your chance of winning? Enter your highest maximum bid. eBay will only use as much of your bid as necessary to win. You could end up paying much less than you think.

Title: COLLINS FRENCH to ENGLISH DICTIONARY, 1CD £30

Time left:	3 days 12 hours
History:	6 bids
Current bid:	£3.00
Your new maximum bid:	£ 10.00 (Enter £3.20 **or more**)

[Bid Again >]

How did this... were outbid

How does... your maximum you'll have to

Reminder: winning bidd the status of

8

Yes. I am now the current leader. The important thing here is that my bid stands at £7.01, not £10. This tells me that the hidden proxy must have been £6.51. Why? Because the bid increment for items priced between £5.01 and £15 is 50p, and eBay has automatically bid 50p over the next highest bid. Meanwhile, I get an email confirmation of my bid and status. The bidder that I have just beaten gets one too. He knows that he is no longer in the lead.

Bid Confirmation

Hello kyle216363! (Not you?)

✓ **You are the current high bidder**

Important: Another user may still outbid you, so check this item again before it ends. eBay will send you an email if you're outbid.

Title: COLLINS FRENCH to ENGLISH DICTIONARY, 1CD £30

Time left:	3 days 12 hours
History:	7 bids
Current bid:	£7.01
Your maximum bid:	£10.00

9

Let's now view this auction from an outsider's viewpoint. As expected, my User ID is displayed as the highest bidder and the current price stands at £7.01. Anybody who wants to bid on this item will now have to bid at least £7.51. This, of course, won't be enough: the auction price will simply jump to £8.01 in my favour. eBay will continue to increase my bid right up to my £10 maximum. However, right now nobody knows that my £7.01 is backed by a proxy.

COLLINS FRENCH to ENGLISH DICTIONARY, 1CD £30

You are signed in

Go to larger picture

Current bid:	£7.01
	[Place Bid >]
Time left:	**3 days 11 hours**
	10-day listing
	Ends 28-Oct-04 22:07:56 BST
	Add to Calendar
Start time:	18-Oct-04 22:07:56 BST
History:	7 bids (£0.99 starting bid)
High bidder:	kyle216363 (0) 8

The bid history link reveals what we already know: my current proxy bid is £7.01 and the previous hidden proxy was £6.51. The question now is whether the beaten bidder or anybody else will respond. With so much time left to run in the auction, anything might happen.

Item title:	COLLINS FRENCH to ENGLISH DICTIONARY, 1CD £30
Time left:	3 days, 11 hours 53 minutes 37 seconds

Only actual bids (not automatic bids generated up to a bidder's maximum) are shown. Automatic bids may be placed days or more about bidding

User ID	Bid Amount	Date of bid
kyle216363 (0) 8	£7.01	25-Oct-04 10:06:22 BST
████████ (284 ☆)	£6.51	20-Oct-04 22:43:48 BST
kyle216363 (0) 8	£2.80	25-Oct-04 10:04:19 BST
kyle216363 (0) 8	£2.40	25-Oct-04 09:57:57 BST
████████ (283 ☆)	£2.00	22-Oct-04 21:31:57 BST
████████ (6)	£1.50	20-Oct-04 14:11:52 BST
████████ (36 ☆)	£0.99	19-Oct-04 15:55:11 BST

Meanwhile, the item has been automatically added to the Bidding list in My eBay (this happens whenever you place a bid). The Bidding link in the sidebar provides a summary of the auction action. My £10 proxy bid is displayed here but only I know what it is. I can forget about this item for a while...

With a little under seven hours left, somebody places a bid but is beaten by my proxy. The price jumps to £8.05. Will my £10 maximum be sufficient to win the day and the dictionary?

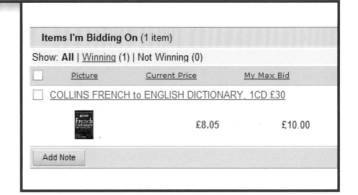

Nope. I have been outbid and receive confirmation via email from eBay. I could bid again – there's plenty of time – or I could lick my wounds. What would have happened if I'd played my cards closer to my chest and saved my £10 bid until the very end of the auction? Perhaps I could have won with a late bid. Perhaps my early proxy merely inflated the price.

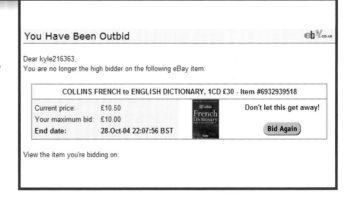

The auction finally ends on £11, as I can see on My eBay, and we'll never know what might have happened. But it should be clear that nothing is gained by bidding early. If the auction would have gone higher than my maximum in any case, then I lost nothing. If it had stayed at under £10 until the end, as it may well have done, I could have had myself a bargain.

A summary so far

The problems with the previous example are clear. You might win an auction by placing an incremental bid or an early proxy bid but the chances are that you will not. Here's a summary of the pitfalls.

- An incremental bid can be beaten instantly by a higher, hidden proxy.

- A winning incremental bid puts you at the lead in an auction… but so what? All you have done is reveal your hand as an interested party. You can still be beaten at any time.

- If you rely on incremental bids, you may run out of time even if there is no hidden proxy at play. Unless you are logged in and actively bidding in the final minutes and seconds, you can be trumped at the death by anybody who's faster on the button. Worse, you can be beaten at a price well below your true maximum.

- Placing a true maximum proxy bid is smarter. You still have to reveal your hand as a player but eBay does all the hard work and automatically raises your bid as and when necessary to keep you in the lead. Nobody knows how high you are prepared to go unless and until they breach your proxy.

- However, when an eBayer gets beaten by a proxy bid, he may well keep bidding until he beats you. This is natural behaviour: we all like to be in pole position. But the net effect is merely to drive up the price. In other words, you could end up losing an auction that you could otherwise have won within your true maximum price.

- If you're lucky, a bidder will walk away after being outbid once or twice by a hidden proxy. If nobody is prepared to bid against an 'invisible enemy', you might win the auction easily. But only if you're lucky and only if it's an auction of little general interest.

As we said earlier, the best strategy is to place a proxy bid that reflects your true maximum price, but to place it very late in the day. This is the essence of sniping. The benefits?

- If your true maximum is some way higher than the current price, you cannot be beaten by an incremental bid. There simply won't be time for other bidders to reach and breach your proxy. They probably won't have time even to push the price up.

- If your true maximum is only just above the current price, you may be outbid by a late incremental bid. In this case, and only in this case, we would suggest pushing your maximum to just above the next incremental level. Ideally, go two bids higher. For instance, if the current price is £10 with seconds left, an incremental bid of £10.50 would win but could be beaten at the death by £11. If your maximum is £11, bid £11.13 or some such random figure to beat both bids without going over the top.

You may find that your last-second proxy bid is beaten by an earlier, higher proxy. Too bad. Equally, somebody might bid higher at the same time as you. Ditto. But the point is that these bids *were going to happen anyway* (or indeed had *already* happened in the case of an earlier proxy). You haven't artificially inflated the auction price by bidding early. So long as the current price is below your true maximum, you can only lose to somebody who is genuinely prepared to pay more for the item than you.

Let's see sniping in action.

PART  Manually sniping an auction

For this example, we'll find a cheapish but popular item and make a last-moment bid to try to grab it from under the noses of earlier bidders. Sniping is a growing trend on eBay and it's a strategy better mastered than ignored.

I'm looking for a 256MB or 512MB USB flash drive for my computer. By searching eBay for recently closed auctions (see Step 4 on p73), I establish that the going prices are £20–30 and £25–40 respectively. That's quite some range.

128Mb USB FLASH MEMORY KEY PEN DRIVE – NEW	£11.27	10
256Mb USB FLASH MEMORY KEY PEN DRIVE – NEW	£20.01	13
512Mb USB FLASH MEMORY KEY PEN DRIVE – NEW	£31.00	13
256MB USB Flash Disk / Pen / Memory / Key Drive New	£21.99	1
256MB USB FLASH MEMORY KEY / PEN DRIVE BRAND NEW SEALED	£23.01	18
EASY DISK 256MB USB 2.0 FLASH DRIVE MEMORY KEY PEN UK	£17.00	8

Here's a 512MB model priced at £29 with 11 minutes left on the clock. I optimistically decide that I'll go as high as £33. Postage will set me back a further £4.50. I could place my bid now as a proxy ... or I could wait. I choose the latter course.

512Mb USB FLASH MEMORY KEY PEN DRIVE – NEW
You are signed in

Current bid:	£29.00
	Place Bid >
Time left:	**11 mins 46 secs**
	1-day listing
	Ends 25-Oct-04 16:32:34 BST
Start time:	24-Oct-04 16:32:34 BST
History:	19 bids (£0.99 starting bid)
High bidder:	(I)

Go to larger picture

I stay on the item page and use my browser's refresh button to periodically update the onscreen information. If you don't do this, you won't see any price changes. With seven minutes left, the price leaps to £33.50 and I'm beaten before I begin. That's eBay. It sells for £38.50.

512Mb USB FLASH MEMORY KEY PEN DRIVE – NEW
You are signed in

Current bid:	£33.50
	Place Bid >
Time left:	**6 mins 58 secs**
	1-day listing
	Ends 25-Oct-04 16:32:34 BST
Start time:	24-Oct-04 16:32:34 BST
History:	20 bids (£0.99 starting bid)
High bidder:	(5)

Go to larger picture

Back to the search page again (I saved my initial search for flash drives as described on p43) and I find an identical item with the same seller currently selling at £30. There are 10 bids and 25 minutes left. However, the high bidder's User ID looks familiar. By comparing the bid histories, I spot that this bidder was the second highest bidder in the previous auction. He went to £37.50 and, having lost once, will presumably go just as high or higher this time around. I'd rather not be up against him.

So I find an alternative USB drive. This one currently stands at £28.75 with 19 minutes left. I reflect that my initial £33 maximum might not cut it this particular afternoon and resolve to go to £38. Again, I can bid now and force the hands of other bidders ... or I can bide my time. I add the item to my watch list lest I should lose track of it.

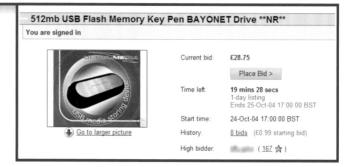

6

Two minutes later, the price stands at £31. I check the bid history and, sure enough, my earlier nemesis is leading the race. He now leads at least two auctions that I am interested in. As is my right, I indulge in a spot of shadowing and establish that he has bid on no

fewer than five auctions for 512MB USB flash drives, all of which end soon. He's clearly keen but it's a risky business for he could conceivably end up winning the lot. See p107-108 for a *better, risk-free approach.*

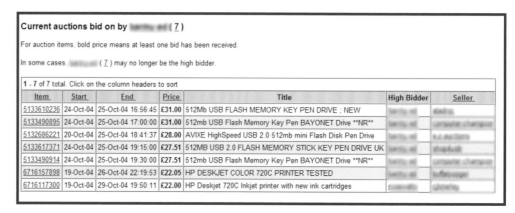

7

I keep an eye on the auction from Step 5, which I've also added to my watch list. To make life easier, I do this from My eBay. Here I can monitor the progress of both auctions. They both stand at £31, one with seven minutes to go and the other with ten. It's nail-biting stuff. My mystery opponent is no longer leading either race.

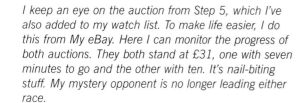

Remember to refresh the page regularly to see the latest information. With two minutes left to run in the earlier auction, the prices stand at £33. I suspect that my revised £38 maximum might just be enough. It's certainly a good day for USB flash drive sellers.

The first auction is over, with the drive selling for £35.50. My opponent was not the highest bidder and nor is he currently leading the other auction that I'm watching. Maybe he's won a drive elsewhere? No time to check – it's now or never. With two minutes left on the clock, I click Bid Now.

This takes me to the Place a Bid page. I enter £38.13 – it's always sensible to go a little higher than a regular increment to minimise the risk of duplicate bids – and click Place Bid. Be warned that eBay may ask you to re-enter your password at this point, which eats into the little time remaining.

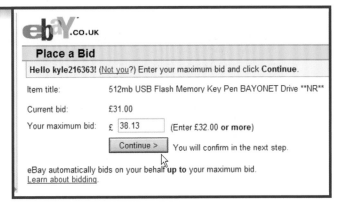

eBay immediately confirms that I am the highest bidder at £36.50. There's hardly any time left and there's obviously no higher proxy in place, for otherwise I would have been instantly and automatically outbid. Surely, this time, the flash drive is mine?

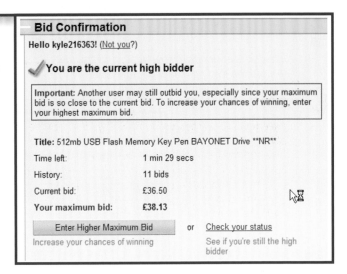

I return to My eBay to watch the close. With under one minute, I lead the auction. If somebody bids *incrementally, they'll only get to £37.50 and I'll still win. Perhaps I can't lose?*

Oops. Sniped! The auction ends and the drive sells for £39.13 to somebody else. An email arrives to tell me the same but it's too late to bid again even if I wanted to. Somebody – and you can guess who – trumped me at the death. I console myself with the fact that I *wouldn't have paid higher than £39.13 under any circumstances, but can't help thinking that I gave other bidders just too much time to manoeuvre. In an eBay auction, twenty seconds is too long.*

I shadow the winning bidder again and see that he's still the leading bidder on three auctions for almost identical items. My guess is that he will no *longer be interested in upping his bids, given that he now owns a drive. This encourages me to add these three items to my watch list.*

As always, I check the terms and conditions of the sale carefully and read the seller's feedback. This narrows the target list to a single item. It is, in fact, an identical product being sold by the same trader. With two hours left, it stands at £27.51. I make a note to return to my computer later... And then realise that I can't because I'm going out. If only, I might muse, it was possible to place a late bid automatically even when away from your computer (see p110).

When the auction ended in Step 13, eBay sent me a notification email. This contains links to similar items currently on auction. For instance, there are several other USB flash drives on offer. In fact, I could snap up a 512MB model for the Buy It Now price of £36.99, which is less than my high bid earlier. If this shows anything, it's simply that it's all too easy to pay over the odds when you find yourself up against a determined bidder.

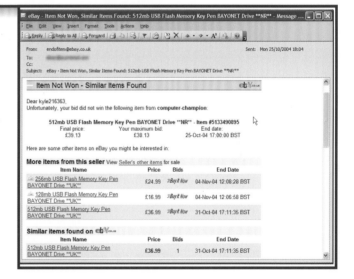

Click the links in the eBay email to view the auction pages for the items. However, do not assume that eBay in any way endorses the seller or warrants the suitability of the item. When you lose an auction, it's tempting to grab the next best thing and perhaps forget to check the seller's feedback with your usual scrupulousness. This would be seriously unwise. In this example, it turns out that one of the sellers has had a spate of recent negative feedbacks. This is certainly sufficient to make me look elsewhere.

No corespondance, no goods, Have reported to ebay and paypal. DO NOT DEAL WITH!		Buyer
Still no communication from seller 8 weeks after payment made.		Buyer
Fast delivery, would buy from again.		Buyer
Thanx, packed well, quick delivery.		Buyer
good communication, nice, easy transaction - thanks!		Buyer
excellent		Buyer
Gds not recvd-No response to emails-Phone # supplied by ebay disconnected.		Buyer

PART 4 Snipe to win

Let's explore last-second sniping a little further. As we saw in Steps 10–13 on p103-104, placing a bid at the end of an auction is a bit of a palaver. You have to be sitting at your computer and quick with the clicks, but you are still vulnerable to a faster, or a later, bidder. Automated sniping is where a third-party service places a bid on your behalf. Essentially, it's just smart software.

Ripe for a snipe?

The thing to remember about any form of sniping, automatic or manual, is that it works best in low-interest auctions. Where there are many interested parties, bidding is likely to get out of hand and the eventual selling price may well go much higher than your true maximum. In such cases, sniping is useless.

However, where it works brilliantly is when an item has been ticking along or even staying static but suddenly springs into action in the dying minutes. An item priced at £5 for seven days can easily rocket to £20 or more in a matter of moments, buoyed along by frantic incremental bids and hidden proxies. The point of sniping is that you can place a proxy bid in the very last seconds.

Now, just to be crystal clear here, let us emphasise that sniping is not some magic guarantee of success. To win an auction with a snipe, several factor have to hold:

● The timing of your snipe must be so near the close that nobody else has time to beat your bid.

● Your snipe must be higher than the current auction price.

● Your snipe must better any hidden proxy bids.

● If an identical snipe is placed, eBay favours the earlier bid, even if only by a second. This might seem to indicate that you should snipe earlier rather than later. However, we feel it's better to avoid snipe snaps by bidding an odd amount e.g. £20.87 rather than £20 or £20.50.

● To win an auction is one thing; to win it at the right price is something else. Your snipe should reflect your true maximum and not a penny more. Your true maximum is the amount that you are genuinely prepared to pay for the item, excluding

To a sniper, the time remaining in any auction is key.

Sort by:	Time: ending soonest ⌄		Customise Display
Price	**Bids**	**PayPal**	**Time Left ▲**
£18.99	- ≡Buy It Now	🅿	28m
£16.99	- ≡Buy It Now	🅿	55m

postage and packing (although you should factor these costs in when working out your bid).

Of course, you can still be beaten by a higher snipe, just as you can lose any auction to a higher bidder. But you won't be beaten by running out of time, and your bid won't fuel the auction. True, it may push up the final price by eating into another bidder's proxy – for instance, a losing £50 snipe will force a bidder with a higher proxy to pay £55 – but that's not your problem.

In summary, to snipe an auction is to place a one-time-only proxy bid at the last possible moment, thereby showing your hand only when you have to, side-stepping any bid frenzies and leaving nobody any time to react. Come the end of an auction, *if it's possible to win at a given price*, sniping is the surest way to do just that.

And there's more …

Hedging your bets with bid groups

As we saw in the previous example when I tried and failed to buy a USB flash drive, I was up against an opponent who was bidding on several auctions. As a tactic, this has one advantage and one disadvantage: sooner or later, you'll win an item, but you may end up winning two or more items when you only want the one.

Now, you may wonder why the bidder wouldn't simply withdraw other outstanding bids as soon as he wins an item in one auction. The reason is that he can't: eBay does not let you retract a bid. Or rather, it does, but only under certain circumstances (see p140-142). Bid retraction is something to avoid.

However, with sniping you only bid at the last moment, so it's possible to decide not to bid at any time prior to this. Some sniping services automate the whole process for you. This means you can set up snipes on several similar or identical items simultaneously – a practice called group bidding – but have subsequent snipes automatically cancelled as soon as you win your first auction. In the USB flash drive example, I could have placed a £33 snipe on three auctions. I would have lost the auctions that rose to £35.30 and £39.13 but I would probably

Third-party tools like Auction Sniper – http://uk.auctionsniper.com – came into being because an eBayer got fed up with being beaten to the post by somebody with quicker fingers (or a faster internet connection).

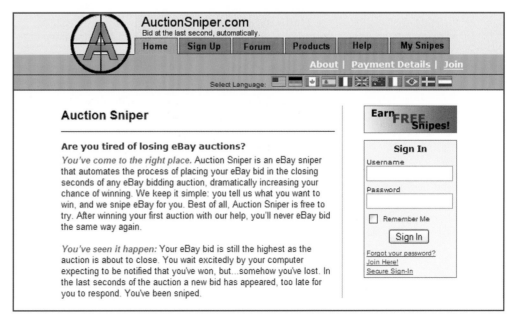

have won the third auction. The drive sold in my absence for £31.62 but my £33 snipe would have pinched it for me for £32.62 (i.e. the minimum bid increment of £1 above the next highest bid). In fact, the only way I could have lost would have been if there was a higher hidden proxy already in place.

Group bidding is thus an effective way to buy a common eBay commodity. You can set your maximum relatively low and hope that eventually you'll snaffle a victory (perhaps at 3am when everybody else is asleep). It also works particularly well when a trader that you trust has multiple auctions for the same product. This saves you the bother of checking lots of different feedback, asking questions of sellers and factoring in different shipping costs. In other words, if a seller has 15 USB flash drives for sale at any one time, you can set up a group snipe bid for the lot and virtually guarantee yourself the best possible price.

On the downside, you have to pay a small commission or fee to use a snipe service – but only if you win. On the upside, sniping can save you money. Let's put one service to the test.

Sniping a single item

For this example, I decide to bid for a newly released Greatest Hits album from Robbie Williams (I needed to buy a birthday present, honest). The second-hand market for this title is virtually non-existent at the moment so I'm looking more to traders with access to new stock than individuals. Or, I suppose, music fans who made a terrible mistake by buying the album and now want to recoup the loss.

A little searching throws up some 80 hits. My first task, as always, is to check the various sellers' feedback, payment terms and postage costs. With such a high demand item, the potential for fraud is relatively high so I resolve to deal only with established traders with excellent feedback. I could Buy It Now for as little as £8.99 plus £3 P&P, which is significantly better than the recommended retail price of £15.79, but I hope to do better in a no reserve auction.

By searching on recently closed, or finished, auctions (see p73), I can see that this CD tends to sell for between £10 and £12 excluding P&P. I want to pay no more than £12.00 including P&P – equivalent to the Buy It Now price – so I find a few auctions that meet my criteria and add them to my watch list in My eBay (see p84). This step is critical.

It's time to register with a sniping service. I'll use Auction Sniper in this example. You have to supply your eBay login name and password, for the service has to be able to access your account directly to place your snipes.

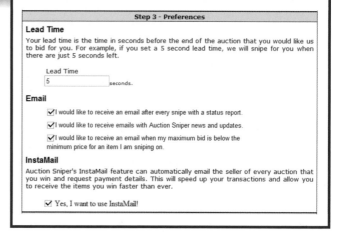

Register with Auction Sniper

Are you tired of losing auctions? Then you've come to the right place. Auction Sniper dramatically increases your chances of winning by automatically placing your bid in the final seconds of each auction.

Don't have an eBay account yet? Click here to go to eBay, then click the "Register" link at the very top of eBays page.

Click here to use our secure sign-up form.   Click here to see how it works!

Step 1 - Account Information	
eBay Username	
eBay Password	
Confirm Password	*Why do we need this?*
Email Address	

Step 2 - Contact Information
Tired of filling out yet another contact form?
Automatically fill out this form for me!

Put checks against the various email notification options to suit. You'll certainly want to receive an email when you win but you may not want to bother with the outbid notifications. Remember, the essence of sniping is bidding your true maximum, so what does it matter if you are outbid? Leave snipe timing at the five-second default.

Step 3 - Preferences

Lead Time

Your lead time is the time in seconds before the end of the auction that you would like us to bid for you. For example, if you set a 5 second lead time, we will snipe for you when there are just 5 seconds left.

Lead Time
5   seconds.

Email

☑ I would like to receive an email after every snipe with a status report.

☑ I would like to receive emails with Auction Sniper news and updates.

☑ I would like to receive an email when my maximum bid is below the minimum price for an item I am sniping on.

InstaMail

Auction Sniper's InstaMail feature can automatically email the seller of every auction that you win and request payment details. This will speed up your transactions and allow you to receive the items you win faster than ever.

☑ Yes, I want to use InstaMail!

Signing into Auction Sniper, open the My Snipes tab and click Import Wizard. Rather cleverly, Auction Sniper will show you your watch list from My eBay. This is why you should add items to the list before coming here

(Step 2). Let's try a one-off snipe first. I select an auction by checking the box next to the title. Enter a maximum bid and select My Snipes in the folder field. Now click the Import Snipes button at the foot of the page.

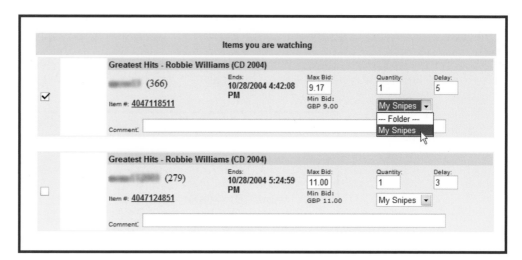

Items you are watching

Greatest Hits - Robbie Williams (CD 2004)

☑ (366) | Ends: 10/28/2004 4:42:08 PM | Max Bid: 9.17 Min Bid: GBP 9.00 | Quantity: 1 | Delay: 5

Item #: 4047118511

My Snipes
--- Folder ---
My Snipes

Comment:

Greatest Hits - Robbie Williams (CD 2004)

☐ (279) | Ends: 10/28/2004 5:24:59 PM | Max Bid: 11.00 Min Bid: GBP 11.00 | Quantity: 1 | Delay: 3

Item #: 4047124851

My Snipes

Comment:

6

When there are five seconds of the auction remaining, Auction Sniper will bid £9.17 on my behalf so long as the auction doesn't rise above this amount in the meantime. I'll get an email if this happens. There are just a few minutes left and the CD stands at £8.50. I suddenly realise that my £9.17 could be beaten by just two incremental bids: £9.00 and then £9.50.

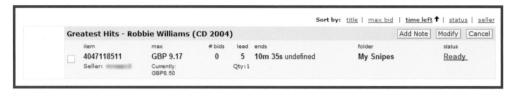

7

Throwing caution to the wind, I put a check in the box next to the auction, click the Modify button and increase my snipe to £9.67. That's better. It'll take three 50p incremental bids or a higher proxy to beat me now. Rather than sit here watching, I can close my browser, turn off my computer and go do something else. So I do. Of course, I'll miss any 'You have been outbid' emails from Auction Sniper but I have no intention of raising my bid.

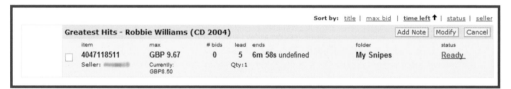

8

Some time later, I return to my computer. In my Inbox are three messages. The first, from eBay, confirms my bid and rather gratifyingly tells me that I'm in the lead. The second, also from eBay, tells me that I've won the auction at £9.50 (so it was worth increasing my bid by that little bit). The third, from Auction Sniper, confirms the same. I am now the proud owner of a Robbie Williams CD, sniped in the last 5 seconds.

9

I complete the payment procedure in the normal manner and wait for my CD. Back in Auction Sniper, the status page under My Snipes tells me what I already know. I now have two successful snipes left to play with before fees kick in, but I can lose for free as often as I like.

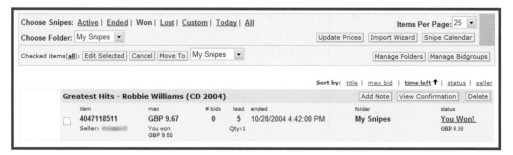

Auction Sniper fees

You never have to pay for an auction that you lose with Auction Sniper and your first three successful snipes are also free. Thereafter, though, you will be asked to register a credit card and billed for each successful snipe. Fees are charged at 1% of the winning price, with a minimum charge of $0.25 and a maximum of $5.00.

Group sniping

The difference this time around is that I'm going to set up a succession of snipes on similar items with the proviso that the sniping will stop – automatically – as soon as I win my first auction.

①

In eBay, add a selection of items to your watch list. As always, check feedback and the terms of sale. If you stick with one trader who is selling the same item in several auctions, as here, you can simplify your life. Otherwise, research each item as seriously as if it was a

one-off purchase. The item that you end up winning may be first, second or tenth on your list. If need be, use the eBay notes feature (p86) to keep track of your maximum purchase price for each item. Remember to factor in the additional post and packing charges and set your bids accordingly.

②

Check how much your target item has sold for in the past (see p73). With flash USB drives (yes, them again) sold by one specialist trader based in the US, I found final prices ranging from $12.06 to

$27.00. I resolve to bid a maximum of $14.35. This would only have won two of six completed auctions shown here but I have to factor in a whopping $16.99 post plus $1.99 compulsory insurance.

	Item Title	Price	Bids
📷	Brand New 256MB USB 2.0 PEN Drive Memory Key 256 MB	US $15.50	9
📷	Brand New 256MB USB 2.0 PEN Drive Memory Key 256 MB	US $20.50	13
📷	Brand New 256MB USB 2.0 PEN Drive Memory Key 256 MB	US $13.75	7
📷	Brand New 256MB USB 2.0 PEN Drive Memory Key 256 MB	US $15.50	9
📷	Brand New 256MB USB 2.0 PEN Drive Memory Key 256 MB	US $12.06	7
📷	Brand New 256MB USB 2.0 PEN Drive Memory Key 256 MB	US $27.00	20
See all items...			

③

Now sign in to Auction Sniper. The trick is to add these items to a 'group bidding' folder rather than the default

My Snipes folder. To do this, open the My Snipes tab and click the Manage Folders button.

④

Give your folder a name and description, and tick the bidgroup box. Now, crucially, select '1' in the field labelled *Bid on the items in this folder until I win*. This ensures that Auction Sniper stops placing snipes as soon as you win one auction. Click *Create*.

⑤

Click *My Snipes* to return to the configuration screen seen in Step 3. Now click *Import Wizard*. This imports all items from your current *My eBay* watch list. Check each item that you want to include in your group, enter a maximum bid and select the bid group folder created in Step 4 from the dropdown menu. Click *Import Snipes* when you're ready.

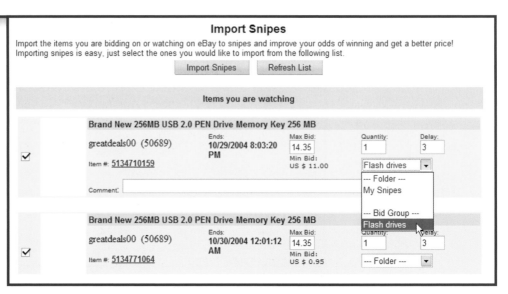

⑥

Back in My Snipes, you can now select your bidgroup folder and see your scheduled snipes listed together. As before, you can modify or delete any entry. That's all you have to do at this stage. Come the end of the first auction, Auction Sniper will place your bid automatically if the price is below your maximum. If you win, all outstanding snipes from this group will be cancelled; if you lose, Auction Sniper will try again on the second auction, and the third, and so on. Feel free to log out of Auction Sniper and eBay.

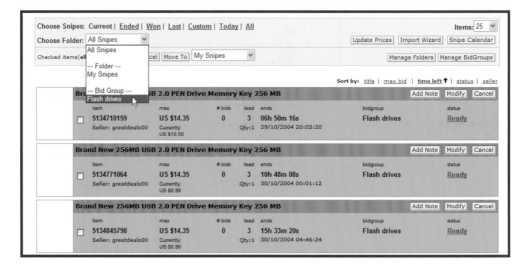

You can keep tabs on your snipes as time goes by and make modifications if necessary. Here, my opening snipe is already a non-starter because the auction has gone higher with over an hour left on the clock. I can up my bid now or write it off and wait for the next snipe to kick in. *Auction Sniper also sends me an 'Outbid Alert!' email the instant a pending snipe is beaten so I should have sufficient notice even if I'm not logged into Auction Sniper or eBay at the time.*

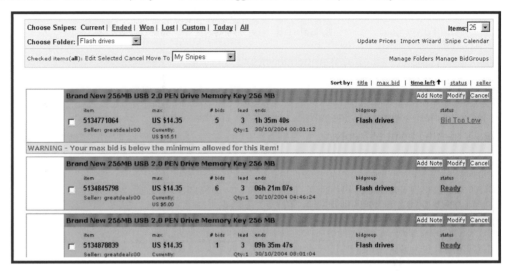

Unfortunately, my $14.35 maximum was not sufficient to win any of the four auctions this time around. One of the drives actually sold for less – $14.01 – but my snipe didn't meet the minimum bid increment and so could not be placed. Oh well, there's always tomorrow. The points to remember are:

● *I didn't ramp up the auction price by showing my hand too early.*

● *None of these auctions were winnable at $14.35 in any case, i.e. if $14.35 was my true maximum, I couldn't possibly have won by not sniping.*

● *I could have increased one or more bids at any point prior to the auction end.*

In short, sniping is a no-lose option. If an auction is winnable at a given price, a last-second snipe is the best way to secure it.

PART  Feedback: to give and to receive

When you complete an eBay transaction, the idea is that both parties leave feedback. You have three choices – positive, neutral or negative – and also the opportunity to leave a short comment. See p45-53 for more on the details and the point of feedback.

Some sellers will give you feedback as soon as you make payment. This is gratifying and, you may think, only right and proper. However, it does leave the seller short of recourse should a buyer prove to be fraudulent or intractable. For instance, the buyer may falsely claim non-delivery or complain that the item was not as described, or find any of a hundred reasons to complain and to blight the seller's profile with neutral or (horrors!) negative feedback. This is why many, perhaps most, sellers wait to get feedback from their buyers before they respond in kind. It's a sound policy, as problems and disputes can usually be resolved amicably to both parties' satisfaction. Always remember that feedback is permanent (but see p116).

When you receive your first feedback for buying an item, your eBay icon grows parentheses and a number. Click this number or your User ID to open your profile page. If your first feedback is positive, eBay also sends you a congratulatory email.

Here's how to leave your own feedback for a seller.

How gratifying – a virtual certificate commemorating your first feedback.

A 100% positive feedback rating (1 out of 1 ain't bad) and a nice comment from an eBay trader. What better way to get up and running?

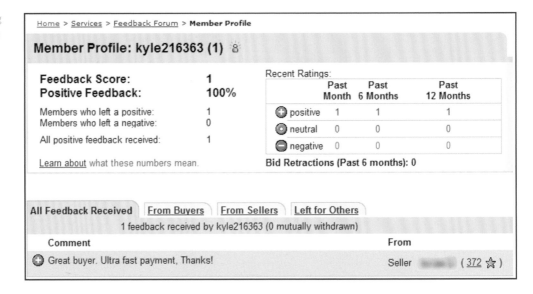

1

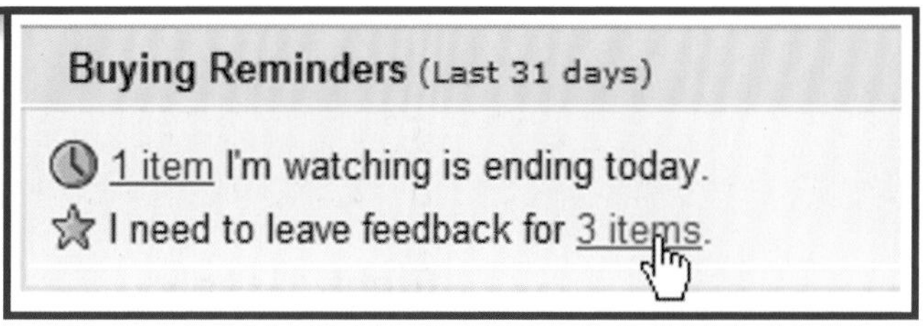

Buying Reminders (Last 31 days)
1 item I'm watching is ending today.
I need to leave feedback for 3 items.

In the Buying Reminders section of your My eBay page, you'll find that eBay keeps prompting you to leave feedback for items that you have won. Here I have three items outstanding. Click the link to see the full selection.

2

Print Customise
Awaiting Feedback
Period: Last 31 days Go
Qty Sale Price Total Price Sale Date Action
1 £17.50 £20.45 31-Oct Leave Feedback
1 £9.50 £11.00 28-Oct Leave Feedback
1 £13.99 £13.99 22-Oct Leave Feedback

Of these items, only the first has actually arrived. I'm happy with the product, or at least with the seller's service and delivery, and I'm thus happy to respond favourably. If I was unhappy, I would be tempted not to leave feedback at all – the risk of retaliation is too great – unless I actively wanted to warn off other bidders. Click the Leave Feedback link.

3

Put a check mark in the Positive box, type a few words and click the Leave Feedback button. Once again, let us emphasise that you cannot retract *feedback, so never leave a message in anger. Equally, we strongly advise you to never leave feedback until you have received the item and checked that it is OK, no matter how nice the seller is. If a seller contacts you to request (or demand) feedback before your item arrives, just say no.*

Feedback Forum: Leave Feedback
help
Every eBay user has a feedback score based on ratings from other members. Feedback lets you reward eBay users and inform the community about your experiences with others. Typically, members give a positive rating if they are happy with a transaction, and a negative when basic obligations have not been met. Keep in mind that what you say about other members becomes a permanent part of their eBay reputation.
Please note:
• Once left, you cannot edit or retract feedback; you are solely responsible for the content.
• It's always best to keep your feedback factual; avoid making personal remarks.
• Feedback can be left for at least 90 days following a transaction.
• If you have a dispute, contact your trading partner to try and resolve the dispute before leaving feedback.
User ID:
Show all transactions
Item Number: 5529770242
Rating: Positive Neutral Negative I will leave feedback later
Comment: Very fast delivery & great communicaton. Highly recommended.
80 chars max.
Leave Feedback

4

All Feedback Received
From Buyers
From Sellers
Left for Others
1871 feedback received by amazing*products (0 mutually withdrawn)
Page 1 of 75
Comment From Date/Time Item #
Very fast delivery & great communicaton. Highly recommended. Buyer kyle216363 (1) 05-Nov-04 10:13 5529770242
Fabulous service and product. Can't wait to see the results. Thank You. xxxxx Buyer (33) 04-Nov-04 21:26 5531420428
Super-fast delivery - Thanks! Buyer (73) 04-Nov-04 18:03 5531420428

Here, on the seller's profile page, my feedback shows up at the top of the list. I have added to the massive, global, public eBay record and done my bit for the community. Hopefully the seller will notice and respond in kind.

Right of reply

If you receive feedback that you know or consider to be unfair, you have a right of reply. From your own feedback profile page, look for the Reply to feedback received link. This leads to a list of all incoming feedback, in which you can find the comment and click the Reply link. Add your side of the story and make it convincing. The thing to remember is that other eBayers will be scouring your feedback in the future and this is your one-time chance to convince potential trading partners that you're neither a rogue nor incompetent.

But don't be rude. The person who left the original feedback then has one further chance to respond, and this response also becomes a matter of permanent, public record. Calling somebody a cretin is unlikely to achieve a happy outcome.

Use your right of reply wisely and only in extremis.

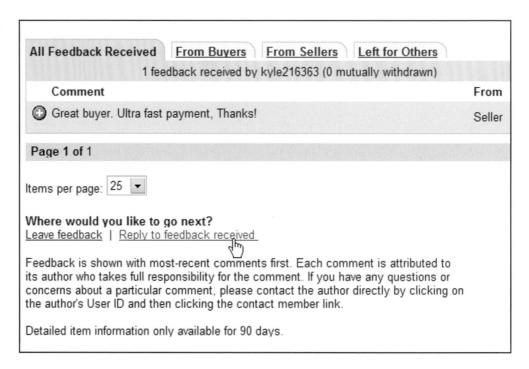

Feedback withdrawal

Inevitably, there are occasions when somebody says something that they later regret and wants to wipe the slate clean. eBay doesn't allow you to retract feedback altogether but, *so long as both parties agree*, it will remove neutral or negative feedback from a member's positive feedback rating. For instance, if you had four trades under your belt where three resulted in positive feedback and one in a negative, your score would be 75%. This is a lousy score. But if you and the feedback leaver can reach an agreement to scrub the negative comment, eBay will deduct it from your feedback score. Your positive feedback score will then return to 100%.

However, *the original comment remains in your feedback profile for all to see*, flagged up as having been mutually withdrawn. Yet again, this emphasises the importance of feedback to each and every eBay member. The upshot is that you should never, ever leave negative (or even neutral) feedback in haste.

All of which being said, note these conditions under which eBay reserves the right to remove feedback completely, 'The feedback comment contains profane, vulgar, obscene or racist language or adult material ... contains personal identifying information about another member, including real name, address, phone number, or email address ... makes any reference to an eBay or law enforcement organization investigation ... [or is] left by a member who provided eBay with false contact information (as verified by eBay).'

To access the mutual feedback withdrawal process, first contact the other member and ensure that you both agree. You both then need to contact eBay directly to lodge the withdrawal request. Search the eBay help menu for 'mutual feedback withdrawal' to access the impossible-to-find form. Or try this link, **http://feedback.eBay.co.uk/ws/eBayISAPI.dll?MFWRequest**.

Act within 90 days of the end of the auction.

Feedback withdrawal happens only by mutual consent.

Feedback Forum: Mutual Feedback Withdrawal

While feedback is a permanent part of member's reputation, ratings left for a particular transaction may be withdrawn through mutual feedback withdrawal. For this to happen, **both members must agree that feedback left is no longer appropriate,** and agree to withdraw using this process. Withdrawn feedback remains in both members' profiles but is no longer counted in the feedback score. Learn More

Before initiating this process, please be sure to contact the other eBay member to resolve any disagreements.

Enter an item number:

[   ]

[Continue >]

When feedback is withdrawn, the original comment and any reply remain in the public domain.

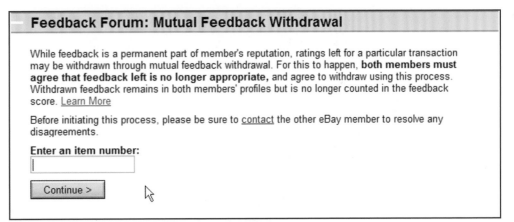

All Feedback Received	From Buyers	From Sellers	Left for Others	
63 feedback received by ▮▮▮▮ (1 mutually withdrawn)				
Comment				**From**
⊕ Prompt payer, smooth sale, credit to Ebay - many thanks !!!!				Seller
⊕ Boots arrived very well packaged...I am thrilled.....Highly recommended !!				Buyer
USER DOES NOT UNDERSTAND HOW EBAY WORKS - I DONT REFUND FOR ROYAL MAIL !!!!! **Reply by** ▮▮▮▮: I do understand, but proof of posting was NOT supplied when requested. **Rating Withdrawn:** Buyer and seller mutually agreed to withdraw feedback for this item. Learn more				Seller
⊕ Payment quickly received, many thanks, Ideal				Seller

PART 5

An eBay seller's guide

Key considerations

Selling stuff on eBay is easy. But your very first consideration should be whether it's really worth your time and trouble. Just because you can sell just about anything on eBay doesn't mean that everything is worth selling on eBay. Sorry to start this section on a downer but here are some of the hassle factors:

Photography In most cases, you'll need to take a photograph of your item. Realistically, this means that you need a digital camera, unless you are prepared to pay to have a traditional film developed and then run the prints through a scanner. Sometimes, you can get away with a 'stock' photo of an item – i.e. an official image, usually found online at a manufacturer's website – but there are copyright implications. Beside, a stock photo will only do for brand new items: if you sell something second-hand, buyers have a right to see the actual item. See Appendix 1 for more on photography.

Postage Because the *buyer* always pays postal charges, along with optional insurance, you won't be out of pocket. However, you should clearly state the cost of post in your auction. This probably means a little research at your local post office. Speaking of which, don't forget that you'll have to package the item and cart it down to your local branch to post it.

Payment An ever-increasing number of buyers expect to be able to use PayPal. This means that you'll need to open your own PayPal account or risk losing a good deal of business. You will also almost certainly need a Premier account unless you are prepared to turn away those who wish to pay with a credit card.

Valuation What is your item actually worth? This may seem a silly question in an auction context – it is, of course, worth whatever somebody is prepared to pay for it and not a penny more – but there are some important implications, as we shall see. You would be very well advised to browse eBay for similar items to gauge the current market value. Don't forget to search for closed as well as current auctions (see p73), as this will give you a better idea of actual prices. Even if your exact item is not listed on eBay, perhaps because it is a genuine one-off, you should still be able to glean some idea of its value.

Factor in the fees Buying on eBay is free but selling is not. There are in fact several fees to pay, depending on which options you select. The main ones are the insertion, or listing, fee which you pay whenever you start an auction and the final value fee, which is a percentage of the eventual selling price. However, there are extra fees for setting a reserve price, including a Buy It Now option, listing your item in more than one category, and all manner of promotional possibilities. For details, see p122-123. Plus, if you accept PayPal, you'll have to pay PayPal's fees.

Communication Just as we encouraged you to ask sellers questions back on p75, so you should expect to receive email queries regarding your own items. You must be prepared to respond to such queries quickly and accurately if you want to be successful on eBay. That is, you can't simply list your item and forget about it for a week or 10 days. At the end of an auction, you will also have to exchange messages with your buyer to co-ordinate payment and perhaps make special shipping arrangements. And then, finally, don't forget the importance of feedback.

After all of this, is it really worth flogging a china horse for £1.50 when your net profit is 2p?

Is the price right?

When you list an item for auction, you have to make some pretty important decisions about pricing and pay fees accordingly. These include:

Starting price Every auction has a starting price, which is simply the lowest bid that you are prepared to accept. It can be as low as 1p. You'll notice from the table below that eBay's insertion fee is based on your starting price so it obviously makes sense to keep this as low as possible. However, you have to bear in mind that you may be forced to sell at that very price. If you start your auction at £0.01 and receive one bid for precisely £0.01, then £0.01 is the selling price. Unless you set a ...

Reserve price This is the price below which you are not prepared to sell. For instance, you can start your auction at £0.01 but specify that you won't sell the item for less than £10. When the first bidder comes along and bids a penny, their bid is accepted but they see a 'Reserve price not met' message. So does everybody else. This can be discouraging in a similar way to a hidden proxy bid in the sense that nobody knows how high the reserve price is until they actually reach it. In other words, it puts the onus on buyers to bid repeatedly. Many won't bother. Many more will walk away at the first sign of a reserve and look for no-reserve auctions for a similar item. Reserve prices are, in a word, off-putting.

Moreover, you can't use a low starting price plus a high reserve price to economise on fees – e.g. start at a 50p but sell only at £50 or above – because eBay collects a surcharge for reserve price auctions (again, see the table below). However, this fee is refunded if your item reaches the reserve and sells. We believe it's better to keep buyers interested and involved by using the starting price as the main means of price control, not a reserve. If you really hope to raise £50 from an auction, then set your *starting price* at £30 or £40 and hope for the best. Don't bother with a reserve price at all. True, if you set the starting price too high, you risk scaring off bargain hunters, but you'll scare off more with a 'reserve price not met' handicap.

Final value When your item sells, you pay eBay a commission. If your item doesn't sell, you pay nothing.

Buy It Now If you want to include a Buy It Now price in order that a bidder can end your auction early – see p88-89 for details – you must pay an additional fee. If you want to make your auction Buy It Now-*only*, in which case it's no longer an auction at all, you pay the equivalent of the final value fee. That is, you'll

Fluffy carpets are *de rigueur* when photographing items for eBay.

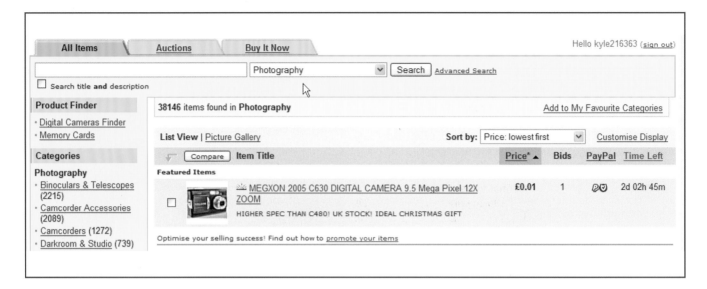

If you're prepared to pay a little bit extra, eBay will give your item preferential display status. This camera is a 'Featured Plus!' item, which means the seller paid £9.95 to have it listed at the top of the page.

pay the same final value fee for a £10 Buy It Now-only listing as for an item that sells for £10 in open auction.

Additional category We saw back on p32-34 how eBay auction items are listed in categories. This means that it's possible for a buyer to find items of interest by browsing categories rather than (or as well as) using search keywords. Any item you list for auction appears for free in one category only, but you can list in a second category if you like. This can help to increase your market reach, particularly if your item falls naturally into two camps. For instance, an antique teddy bear could as easily be listed in the Collectible category as in Dolls & Bears.

eBay charges double the listing fee for this. And if you set a reserve price, this fee is doubled, too. However, the reserve fee will be refunded if the item sells.

Beyond all of the above, you can choose to pay additional fees for optional extras. For instance, by default an eBay auction finishes at the same time as it starts, albeit several days later. If you happen to list an item at 1.30am on a Wednesday morning but figure you'd get more last-minute action if the auction closed at 2pm on a Saturday afternoon, you can pay 12p to choose the closing time. This is known as a 'scheduled listing'.

You can also pay to have a thumbnail picture of your item on search result pages, to have your auction title emboldened, or for your auction to appear in one of eBay's featured promotions. The key point to remember is that a buyer will find your item regardless so long as you list and describe it appropriately, so we're disinclined to pay over the odds for bells and whistles.

eBay fees

eBay pricing is not exactly a model of transparency but these are the current prices at the time of writing:

Insertion fee

Starting or reserve price	Fee
£0.01–£0.99	£0.15
£1.00–£4.99	£0.20
£5.00–£14.99	£0.35
£15.00–£29.99	£0.75
£30.00–£99.99	£1.50
Over £99.99	£2.00

Reserve price fee (refunded if the item sells)

Reserve price	Fee
£0.01–£49.99	Free
£50.00–£4,999.99	2% of the reserve price
£5,000.00 and up	£100.00

Final value fee

Closing price	Fee
Item not sold	None
£0.01–£29.99	5.25% of the winning bid
£30.00–£599.99	5.25% of £29.99 (£1.57) plus 3.25% of the remaining value of the winning bid
Over £600.00	5.25% of £29.99 (£1.57) plus 3.25% of £569.99 (£18.53) plus 1.75% of the remaining value of the winning bid

Other fees

Service	Fee
Buy It Now	£0.06
Additional category	Double the insertion fee (and reserve fee, if applicable)
Scheduled listing	£0.12
Item subtitle	£0.50
Additional pictures	£0.12 each

Counting the cost

What we need here is an example. Let's say you sell a first edition of a book for £70. Here are how the fees might pan out.

You start the bidding at £25 with a £55 reserve. Your fees are thus:

- **Insertion** £0.75
- **Reserve** £1.10
- **Final value** £2.87

However, the reserve fee is refunded if the item sells so your total fees come to £3.62. If the book failed to sell at or above the reserve price, you would still have to pay the insertion and reserve fees, so you'd be out of pocket by £1.85.

Let's say you took the view that the book really needed a subtitle, a dual-category listing and a total of four pictures. You don't bother with a reserve price and, because you are confident that the book will sell, you start the bidding at only £3.00. Again, it sells for £70.

This time, your fees would be:

- **Insertion** £0.20
- **Additional category** £0.20
- **Subtitle** £0.50
- **Additional pictures** £0.36
- **Final value** £2.87

This comes to a grand total of £4.13. Would the book have sold anyway without the optional extras? And would it have sold for the same price? That's the mystery of eBay.

PART 5 Item titles

The two most important things to get right as an eBay seller are your item title and description. Most buyers find items by searching on keywords rather than by browsing categories and a default eBay search looks only at titles, not descriptions. The onus is thus on you to include all the relevant keywords in the title if you want people to find it.

Always try to include options for alternative spellings in your item title

Account for inaccuracies

Let's say that you have a Canon digital camera to sell. The item title could look something like this:

Canon PowerShot A75 digital camera

This means that anybody searching on keywords **canon**, **powershot**, **a75** or **digital camera** will find your item. However, that's only half the story. The problem – and it's a real one – is that people don't necessarily search for the right key words. In this example, your camera will be missed by anybody searching for **cannon** instead of **canon**, or for **power shot** instead of **powershot**.

The trick is to try to factor in as many variations as possible. However, you only have 45 characters to play with in your auction title. There are two possible approaches. First, cram as much into your title as possible. For example:

Canon (cannon) PowerShot (power shot) A75

That's 41 characters. It may look ungainly but that alone won't stop people clicking on your item and finding out more. Experienced eBayers will also immediately understand your reasoning and tactic.

Secondly, use the description. You have almost unlimited space to describe your item in full on the auction page so you can include every conceivable mis-spelling or alternative description. However, this is only useful when buyers use the 'search titles and descriptions' option. They may do so, but usually only if a titles-only search fails to throw up a good selection. With a common commodity like a digital camera, potential buyers will likely find many suitable items on their first attempt.

You might think – we did, anyway – that subtitles would be included in a titles-only search. For instance, you could use:

Canon PowerShot A75 digital camera
cannon power shot power-shot 75 digicam compact lightweight

Unfortunately, despite charging 50p for the privilege of running a subtitle, eBay does *not* include subtitle terms in a titles-only search.

The best approach, then, is to include any obvious wrong or alternative spellings in the title if you can, and throw the rest into the description. The worst approach is to assume that people will search 'correctly'. We promise you that they won't. For example, somebody looking for a Winnie the Pooh teddy bear might search on any or all of the following terms (these are all real examples):

- Whinnie
- Winny
- Winie
- Poo
- Tedy
- Teddie
- Bare

Your task as a seller is to help this potential buyer find *your* Pooh bear (or Poo Bare) in the crowd, regardless of their spelling difficulties.

PART 5 Item descriptions

Be scrupulously honest, accurate and comprehensive when describing an item for sale on eBay. Nothing upsets a buyer more than an item that arrives in a worse condition than the description mentioned, or is materially different in any way, or which fails to live up to expectations – and nothing is more likely to lead to a claim for a refund or negative feedback. Even if you consider that the buyer should know something or other about your item – you may consider it common knowledge (and common sense) that an MP3 player described as 'capable of storing 40,000 songs' will not actually be *supplied* with 40,000 songs pre-loaded – it does no harm to make this explicit.

Picture this

Photographs should also be used to illustrate your items. Never, ever conceal a flaw with a crafty photograph angle or fail to mention it in the description. For instance, when I sold an old Gameboy recently, I was concerned about some light scratching on the screen. Try as I might, I could not capture these scratches in a photograph. I thus decided to explain this issue in the item description:

There is some light, superficial scratching on several parts of the screen and a more substantial scratch in the extreme upper-right corner. Does this affect gameplay? My 7-year old son claims never to have noticed the scratches (although he would say that, wouldn't he, being personally responsible) and I can honestly say that they don't bother me. But please do be aware that this GBA is not in perfect condition. It has been played with extensively for over a year and treated casually. All of which being said, it works just fine, with no problems that I am aware of. I have a clip-on light (not pictured) which I'll include in the purchase. Sorry, no box or manual.

I considered that my description was accurate and fair but I also privately decided that I would refund the winning bidder if they weren't entirely happy with the item (although I didn't want to advertise this fact on eBay). In the event, the item sold for a good price and I received the following feedback:

Item as described. No problems. Recommended.

It may look fine but there was obvious scratching on the screen. Never try to hide a flaw.

Easy on the hyperbole

There's a related aspect to descriptions which goes beyond all of this; namely making claims on behalf of an item. You know the kind of thing: 'Fantastic performance'; 'The best XYZ on the market'; 'Lose 24 kilos in 48 hours'; 'Immortality Absolutely Guaranteed!!!' and so forth. Be very, very wary of making such claims. Even if you think your item is the best thing since sliced bread, you should separate objective criteria ('30GB hard disk') from personal opinion ('The best MP3 player bar none'). Leave hyperbole to the high street and restrict your descriptions to the plain facts regarding its specification, current condition and purpose. It's up to bidders to research the item independently, not up to you to convince them that it's super-brilliant.

You also have to state your terms of sale, acceptable payment methods, postal costs and whether or not you are prepared to ship overseas and/or offer insurance. However, eBay makes all of this straightforward at the point of listing an item. Let's work through an example now.

You don't want to overstate the merits of your product if there's a risk of customer dissatisfaction.

PART ⑤ Listing an item the EAN way

Truth is, I'm not a big Robbie Williams fan and the CD I
bought back on p110 remained unopened and unplayed.
So why not sell it on eBay?

①

*Log in to eBay and either follow the Sell your item link
or click the large Sell button near the top of the page.
They lead to the same page on which, if this is your first
sale, there are some explanatory links and a further
button to click.*

home | pay| register| sign out | services | site map

.CO.UK | Buy | Sell | My eBay | Community | Help |

Welcome to eBay, kyle216363

You're now signed in to eBay.

Where would you like to go next?
- The item I last looked at
- My eBay
- Sell your item
- View site updates on the Announcement Board

②

*You will now be asked to provide eBay with personal
details and a credit or debit card. If you've already
registered with PayPal, this may seem like a lot of extra
fuss. After all, PayPal is an eBay company. However,
you currently have no choice.*

Seller's Account: Verify Information   Help

① **Verify Information**   2. Provide Identification   3. Select How to Pay Seller Fees

Please have the following ready, as you'll need both to sell on eBay UK:
- Credit or debit card
- Cheque book (bank account)

First, verify that your information below is correct.

First name
Kyle

Last name
MacRae

Street

Town / City
Glasgow

County
Glasgow (City of)

Post code

Country
United Kingdom
Change country

③

*Work through the form. On this page, having just
provided credit card details, I now have to provide my
bank account details for further verification.*

Seller's Account: Provide Check Identification   help

1. Verify Information   ② **Provide Identification**   3. Select How to Pay Seller Fees

Please place a bank account on file. Why? This assures eBay of your identity and increases overall
site safety. eBay will **not** deduct funds from your account unless you authorise us to do so.

Account owner
Kyle MacRae

Bank name
Bank of Scotland
UK bank accounts only
Bank address

Glasgow
Bank postcode

4

Registering to sell items on eBay is free but you will be subject to fees, as discussed earlier. You must now decide how to pay. I'll opt for the credit card option rather than a bank transfer, although it comes to much the same thing.

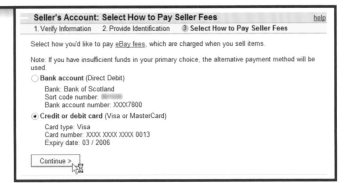

5

That's it, I'm ready to make my fortune. The very first thing to notice is that I can't include a Buy It Now price in my auction. This option is restricted to those who have acquired 10 positive feedbacks. As a beginner, all I can do is run a standard, open auction.

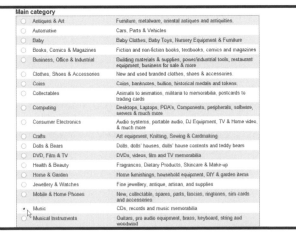

6

First off, I need to pick a category. eBay provides a list of top-level categories, one of which is Music and described as appropriate for 'CDs, records and music memorabilia'. That fits nicely. However, if the correct category for one of your items is not immediately obvious, the easiest thing to do is see what categories other people have used for similar items.

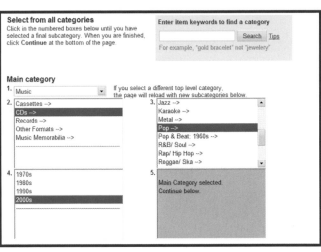

7

I can now select from various sub-categories. In this simple example, my Robbie CD clearly belongs in Music > CDs > Pop > 2000s. I could list in the antique wardrobe category and it would still show up in a search for Robbie Williams CDs, but anybody browsing eBay categories for the latest pop CDs would miss it.

Now here's an interesting development on eBay. As of recently, you can use an item's European Article Number – a 13-digit number used to identify products internationally – to enter an item description automatically. This can be a great time-saver. Here, my Robbie CD has an EAN so it qualifies.

This is the result – a complete item description replete with a stock photograph. I merely have to state whether my CD is new or used. Better still, there's a checkable option to include the album playlist and other pertinent information in my description, all automatically.

I can add my own information, too. This might seem superfluous but eBay makes me say something so I add a few words of my own and make it clear that I'm selling the item without a reserve price. The Preview description link shows you how your item will look for real.

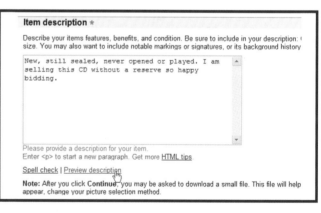

A critical juncture. How low am I prepared to go? The starting price I enter here is the price that I must sell at if I only get one bid. Too high a starting price will put people off; too low risks making a significant loss if the item attracts little attention. A quick check on current auctions for the same CD tells me that the competition favours £8.99. I decide to undercut them with a £5 starting price.

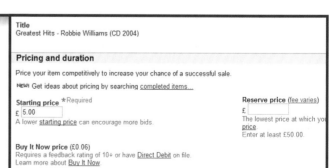

I also decide to make this a 10-day auction and forgo the option to schedule the start and stop times (see p122). Ignoring the many optional extras, including gallery listings, I finally make it to the foot of the page and click Continue.

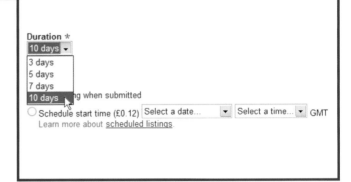

Another critical page. Here I must stipulate which forms of payment I am prepared to accept. Because I have a PayPal account, it makes sense to include it. But do I want to make this a PayPal-only auction? All I have to do is leave every other box unchecked. Against my better judgment but because I want an easy life, this is what I do.

Payment methods *Required
Choose the payment methods you'll accept from buyers.

PayPal

PayPal allows you to accept credit card payments

☑ PayPal (MasterCard VISA AMEX) payment notification will go to: ▓▓▓▓▓▓▓▓
☐ PayPal fees may apply

Other payment methods
☐ Postal Order or Banker's Draft
☐ Personal cheque
☐ Other - See Payment Instructions
☐ Credit Cards
☐ Escrow
    eBay's approved provider is escrow.com

On the same page, I specify how much I'll charge to post the item within the UK. However, because I have also stated that I am prepared to ship the item to Europe, I must follow the Add service link.

Post-to locations *
◉ Will ship to United Kingdom and the following (check all that apply):
☑ Worldwide   ☐ Americas   ☑ Europe   ☐ Asia
              ☐ United States ☑ France   ☐ Australia
              ☐ Canada   ☑ Germany   ☐ Japan
○ Will not ship - local pickup only
    Specify pickup arrangements in the Payment Instructions box below.

Postage costs *
Specify a flat cost for each shipping service you offer.
Domestic Postage (offer up to 3 services)
Royal Mail 1st Class Standard ▾   £ 1.50
Add service | Remove service and have buyers contact me later

International Postage (offer up to 3 services)
Add service

This affords me some choices. The easiest by far is Seller's Standard International Rate, which means I can send the item however I like. I specify £2 for international shipping (a guess). I also decide not to offer insurance for such a low value item. I could say that it's mandatory and charge the seller a stated fee or bump up the post and packing charge, but this puts people off. And frankly, I can't be bothered filling out the forms at the post office.

International Postage (offer up to 3 services)
Select a postage service ▾   £
Select a postage service   ☑ Europe   ☐ Asia
Sellers Standard International Rate   ☑ France   ☐ Australia
Royal Mail Airmail   ☑ Germany   ☐ Japan
Royal Mail Airsure
Royal Mail Surface Mail
Royal Mail International Signed-for
Royal Mail HM Forces Mail
Parcelforce International Datapost
Parcelforce Ireland 24   ...viding a postage cost for your item. It will be displayed to buyers in My eBay.
Parcelforce Euro 48
Parcelforce International Scheduled
Other courier or delivery service   **policy**
Collect in person
                                         Increase sales by offering a postage discount in your description for multiple item purchases.
                                         Describe your return policy and earn buyer confidence. Learn more

Finally, I have the opportunity to add any final thoughts, including details of my refund policy. As I don't actually have one, I leave this section blank save for a polite request for prompt payment. I click Continue.

Payment instructions & return policy

Give clear instructions to assist your buyer with payment, postage and returns.

Increase sales by offering a postage discount in your description for multiple item purchases.

Describe your return policy and earn buyer confidence. Learn more.

I would appreciate payment within 3 days of the auction close, please

Note: 500 character limit.

< Back   Continue >

Up pops a lengthy preview page with full details of my auction listing and the chance to edit each and every section. It's at this point that I notice the listing fee of 35p. If I reduce my starting bid to £4.99, I can save 15p.

I click the Edit pictures and details link on the preview page and make the change. To confirm the new starting price, I click the Save Changes button at the foot of the page. This returns me to the preview page, where my listing fee is now a mere 20p. All that remains now is to click the Submit Listing button and my auction will go live ...

Pricing and duration

Price your item competitively to increase your chance of a successful sale.

NEW! Get ideas about pricing by searching completed items...

Starting price *Required
£ 4.99

A lower starting price can encourage more bids.

Buy It Now price (£0.06)
Requires a feedback rating of 10+ or have Direct Debit on file.
Learn more about Buy It Now.

eBay confirms the listing with an email and I'm up and running. eBay invoices are issued within a few days of the 15th of the month or the last day of the month, depending on when you set up your eBay account. You can pay by credit card, direct debit or, of course, PayPal.

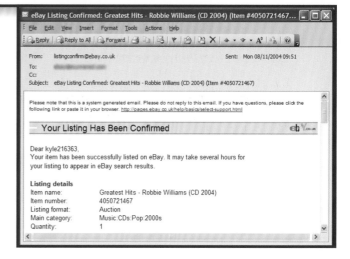

PART 5 **Listing an item manually**

Most items don't come with a convenient EAN number and
eBay doesn't always know about items that do, so usually
you'll have to do the descriptive work yourself. In this
example, we'll start at a point equivalent to Step 8 on p129.

*I'm going to sell a portable external USB hard drive.
This presents me with an immediate problem because
there is one perfect category and one good alternative:
Computing > Components > Storage/Drives > Hard
Drives > 10.1 to 20 GB, and Computing >
Components > Storage/Drives > USB/Pen/Key/Flash
Drives > 512 MB & More. My thinking is that
somebody looking for a lower capacity flash drive might
be tempted by my bulkier but much higher capacity
drive, so I use the second category link and list in both
categories.*

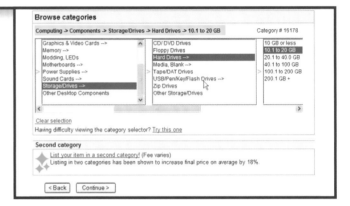

*It's title time. As there are several possible and probable
variations on the drive's proper name, I decide to use a
subtitle to cover the most likely candidates. This should
ensure that somebody searching for this item with
slightly skewed keywords will find it. eBay also invites
me to complete some further fields pertinent to my
category choice.*

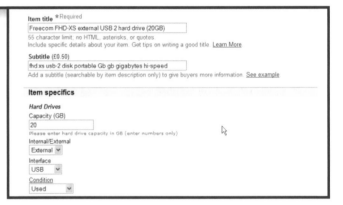

*Lower down the same page, I have the opportunity to
describe my drive in my own words. Now, there are
several approaches here. One is to copy the
specifications from the manufacturer's web page, which
is technically copyright theft; another is to list them in
my own words but perhaps include a link to the
appropriate manufacturer's web page. I adopt the latter
tactic.*

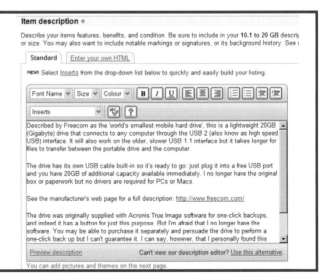

4

You can write your own HTML copy if you like, or simply use the text editor's basic tools for emphasis. Here, for instance, I'm making spartan use of bold, colour and italics. You can easily go wild with design in HTML-mode and you'll see many truly garish eBay auctions on your travels. My personal preference is for simplicity.

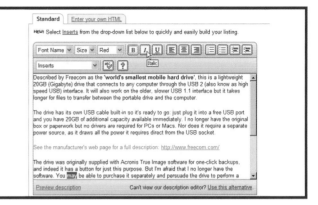

5

Click the Preview description link to see how your description will look on the eBay site, and make any necessary amendments. You will have a further chance to edit your text later. Continue to the next page when you are happy.

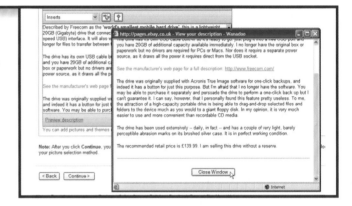

6

As described earlier, enter a starting price, auction duration and, if appropriate, start and end times. You can now also add one or more photos. First time around, eBay will prompt you to download and install a small helper application. This done, which takes only seconds, navigate to your saved photos (see Appendix 1). Of course, I could cheat and use the manufacturer's stock photo but that would be fair to neither the company nor my customers.

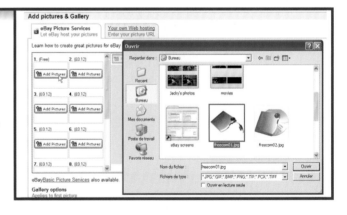

7

I decide that two pictures will suffice, one of which includes a CD to indicate the scale. The second picture will cost me 12p. I can also tick the Gallery option – 15p for this – which means that a thumbnail of the first picture will appear on the search results page (see Step 13).

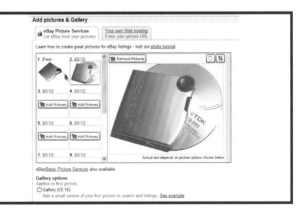

I also select Supersize pictures in order that potential bidders can get a larger, clearer view of my item. This is only worthwhile if your pictures do your item justice, of course, and I'm not at all sure that mine do. Still, it shows a willingness to please. That's another 60p to eBay. Finally, for 7p, I select a theme to jazz up my auction. eBay now uploads my photographs in the background and provides a further opportunity to amend the auction details. You then go to the payment, post and final confirmation pages exactly as before (Step 13 and onwards from p130).

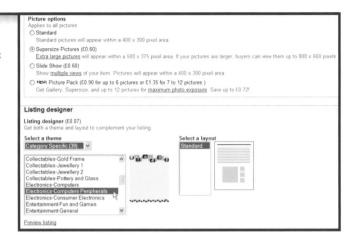

Make any final amendments. With a £50 starting price, my total fees for listing this drive are a whopping £5.88. I'll also be liable to pay a percentage of the selling price. That's not bad for reaching a global audience, but consider this: the insertion, subtitle, additional picture, supersize, gallery and designer fees are all doubled simply because I opted for a double category listing. I could halve my fees at a stroke if I'm prepared to list in just the one category.

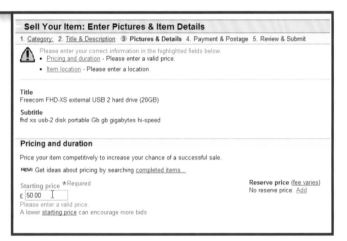

On the basis that most people search on keyword rather than browse by category, I click the Edit Second Category link on this final preview page. I can now click Clear selection and Save Changes to remove the second category altogether.

Main Category	Edit Main Category
Computing:Components:Storage/Drives:Hard Drives:10.1 to 20 GB (#16178)	
Second Category	Edit Second Category
Computing: Components: Storage/Drives: USB/Pen/Key/Flash Drives: 512 MB & More (#51076)	
Title & Description	Edit title & description
See above for preview of title, subtitle, Item Specifics and description.	

My fees are reduced to £2.94. I can click Submit Listing to make my auction go live.

Here is the finished article as it appears in eBay ...

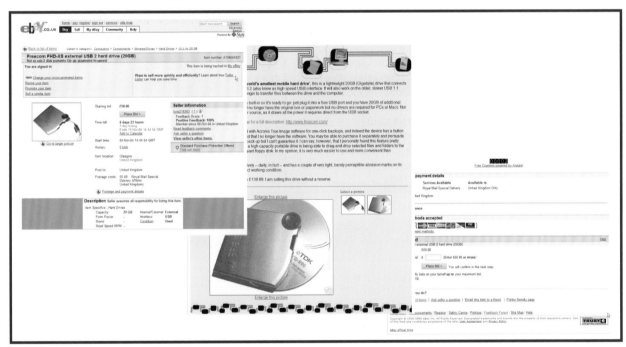

And here is how it shows up when somebody searches for any of the keywords included in my title or subtitle. Note the thumbnail picture alongside the title.

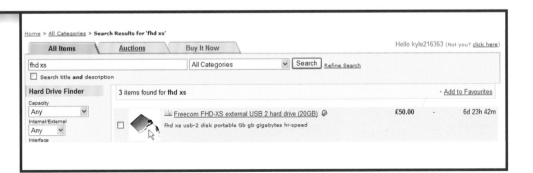

PART ⑤ Monitoring an auction

When you have an auction in progress, you can track it easily from your My eBay page. For instance, here is my Freecom drive auction on the morning after. Some points to note:

Current price If there have been bids, the leading bid will appear here. Do remember that the leading bid is always the next highest bid plus the minimum bid increment. This means that the leading bidder may in fact have placed a much higher proxy bid.

Bids Here you can see how many bids have been placed.

# of watchers Rather fascinating, this one. The number here tells you how many people are currently tracking your item in their own My eBay pages. This is a definite show of interest and it's reasonable to assume that at least some of the watchers will place a bid.

Time left This is simply the time left in days, hours and minutes before the auction closes.

Sell similar Many people routinely sell the same or similar items on eBay. This link is an easy way to start a new auction for the same sort of item. eBay remembers the current settings and applies them by default, leaving you free to make tweaks but saving you the hassle of having to set up categories, pricing and so forth from scratch.

Keep tabs on your auction's progress in My eBay.

Note the little button next to the Sell similar link in the Action column. Click this and you'll see a drop-down menu with several options. The Revise and Add To Description links let you return to your auction listing to make any amendments. You might, for instance, spot a mistake that needs clarification. Or if several people ask you the same question, you might decide that it's worthwhile including the answer in your description.

However, there are limitations:

● *If* your auction has longer than 12 hours to run *and* has attracted no bids, you can change anything. You can edit or completely rewrite the item description. In this case, use the Revise link.

● But if your auction has *either* attracted one or more bids *or* ends within 12 hours, you can only add to (not change) the original description. In this case, use the Add To Description link.

● And if your auction has attracted bids and ends within 12 hours, you can't change a thing.

Confusing it may be, but the upshot is that you are well advised to make changes, particularly factual ones, as early as you possibly can, ideally before your item attracts a bid.

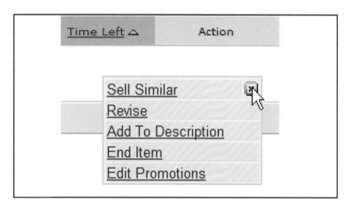

Click here for auction options.

Ending an auction early

There is also an End Item link here but there are conditions for closing a live auction. If the auction has no bids, you can end it easily and immediately but you must tell eBay why. Damaging or losing the item are valid reasons. If there are any outstanding bids, you must cancel them – eBay handles this automatically – or sell the item to the current highest bidder. You can not end an auction within the last twelve hours.

Two things to consider here. Sharp minds may be thinking that it's possible to wait until 13 hours before close and end an auction if it isn't doing particularly well. You may, for instance, be hoping to get £100 for an item but the bidding reaches £50 and stalls. You reckon it won't go much higher. Rather than sell for £50, you pull the item altogether. However, eBay (rightly) considers that this behaviour is the equivalent to reserve price evasion. That is, if you won't sell below £100, you should set a £100 reserve – and pay the corresponding eBay fee. Although you can end an auction early (so long as it has at least 12 hours to run), eBay promises that 'abuse of this option will be investigated'.

A further consequence is that disappointed bidders will be none too pleased with you. Put yourself in their position: you have invested time and energy researching a market, tracked down an attractive item, placed one or more bids, perhaps engaged in a dialogue with the seller – and then suddenly the item vanishes from eBay and you are left high and dry. How many other items have you missed in the meantime because you had your sights set on this one? Will you now have to start the whole process again, perhaps waiting days or weeks for something similar to come along? At the very least, you can expect not to receive bids from these people next time around.

Incidentally, should the current high bidder in an auction contact you and asks you to end the auction early and sell at the current price, be aware that this breaches eBay rules. Say no. You might also be nervous about the chances of receiving payment from such a trader, so consider cancelling his bid (see p140). Should somebody approach you and ask to deal privately outside eBay, say no again and add them to your blocked bidders list (see p143).

If you need to end an auction, act as quickly as possible and tell eBay why.

End My Listing Early

Select a reason for ending your listing early. The reason will appear on the Closed Item page.

- ⦿ The item is no longer available for sale.
- ◯ There was an error in the starting price or reserve amount.
- ◯ There was an error in the listing.
- ◯ The item was lost or broken.

Note: The next page contains a link to provide additional details about why you ended your listing early.

[End My Listing]

Dealing with questions

We saw on p75 how to ask a seller a question, so here we'll look at it from the other side of the relationship. As soon as you have listed an item, any eBay member can send you a direct email. Here's a fairly typical enquiry.

1

I've listed my Robbie Williams CD using the EAN approach described earlier, and described the CD as new, which it is. This eBayer is sceptical, though, and wants me to clarify in black and white that I am selling an original (i.e. legal) CD, not just a home-burned copy. I am happy to reassure him.

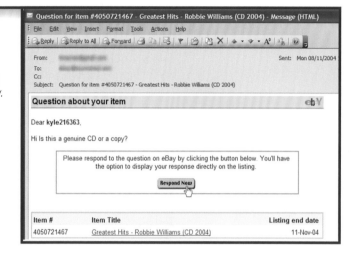

2

The link in the email takes me to an eBay page where I can type a reply. Note the two optional boxes. If you consider that the questioner raised a valid point that would benefit other browsers, you can append the question and your response to your item. You can also opt to keep your email address hidden from the questioner.

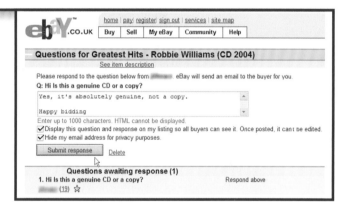

3

We can now see the result on the auction page: the question and my response are there for all to see. Hopefully nobody else will now ask the same question. The rule is to reply to all questions politely, promptly and accurately. If you or a questioner uncovers some vital information that you forgot to mention, revise your description immediately (use the Revise link seen on p137) or check the 'Display this question and my response' box.

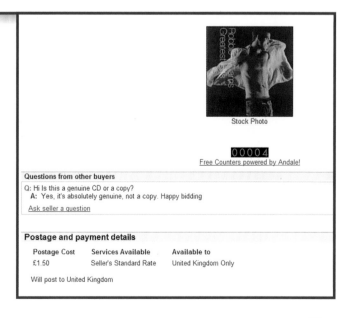

Cancelling a bid

Let's now look at a trickier situation. A bidder has offered a whopping £1.50 for my Robbie Williams CD but has apparently failed to notice my payment terms until it's too late. He doesn't have a PayPal account and so cannot pay for the item should he win.

The central point here is that the bidder has entered into a contract with me and I can oblige him to see it through. If he wins the auction and is unable to fulfil his side of the agreement – i.e. pay for the CD with PayPal – then he could be in breach of contract. Our bidder decides he wants to get out of this pickle. Here's how it might play out:

The bidder goes to his own My eBay page and finds the item he's bidding on (my Robbie CD). He can now click the seller's name to access the feedback profile page.

On this page, there is a Contact Member button. This button only appears because the bidder is already actively engaged in an auction with the seller. If he hadn't placed a bid, the only way to contact the seller would be through the Ask seller a question option discussed earlier.*

Our bidder confesses his problem and asks for a way out of his commitment. In truth, he is very unlikely to win the auction with a bid of £1.50 but perhaps he actually placed a £15 proxy bid.

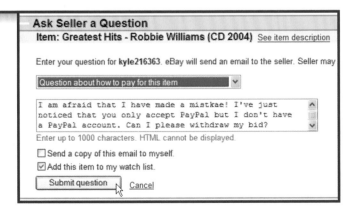

4

In comes the eBay email with a Respond Now button. I consider my options. I could hold fast and insist that the bidder signs up with PayPal, but there's always the chance that he'll simply refuse to pay up and blight me with negative feedback for being unreasonable.

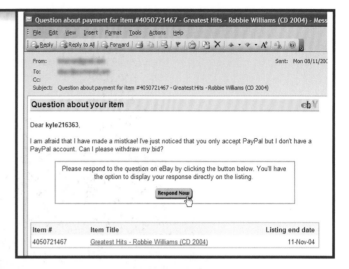

5

I decide to forgive his little lapse and let him off the hook, just as I would if he'd said he'd lost his job and suddenly couldn't afford to pay for the item (or any of 1,001 other plausible excuses). But how to proceed, exactly? The response page doesn't offer any obvious options so I type a positive reply to the bidder in the meantime and explore the eBay Help menu. This time, I don't want the question and response to show up on the auction page.

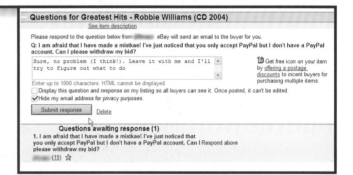

6

There are in fact two ways to revoke a bid. The bidder can complete a Retract Bid form, or the seller can complete a Cancel Bid form. In this particular case, eBay rules (see p142) dictate that bidder does not have a valid reason for retracting the bid so it's up to the seller to cancel. You need to know the item number and the bidder's User ID, both of which can be gleaned from your My eBay page. You must also explain to eBay why you are cancelling the bid. Click Cancel Bid.

7

Voila. eBay confirms that the bid has been cancelled and the bidder is free from his obligation. However, the original bid and its subsequent cancellation remain detailed on the auction's Bid History page for the benefit (whatever that might mean) of other eBayers.

The rules of retraction

eBay has very specific rules regarding bid cancellation and retraction. For the full details, look here –
http://pages.eBay.co.uk/help/buy/questions/retract-bid.html – or search the Help system for 'retract bid'.

Here are the essentials. As a *bidder*, you can retract a bid at any time up until 12 hours before the auction end, but only if:

- You entered the wrong amount by mistake (in which case you must rebid with the correct amount), or ...

- The item description changes significantly after you place the bid. For instance, the seller adds: 'Whoops, I've just noticed that this is a 20GB model, not a 40GB as I said above. Sorry everybody.' or ...

- You cannot contact the seller by email or telephone.

You cannot retract a bid if you took advantage of a Buy It Now offer. If there are under 12 hours of an auction to run, you may only retract a bid within one hour of placing it. Moreover, 'eBay will thoroughly investigate bid retractions. Abuse of this feature may result in the suspension of your account.'

It's also worth noting that bid retractions are logged in your profile. Other eBayers will often take bid retractions as a sign that a trader is unreliable and may decline (or cancel) your bids.

If you need to get out of a commitment, it is far, far better to ask the seller to cancel a bid on your behalf, as in the example given above. A cancelled bid does not blight your profile. Again, though, there are rules. A seller *should* only cancel a bid if:

- A bidder asks him to do so, or ...

- He has tried but failed to verify the bidder's identity.

The second condition is obviously a completely grey area but it gives you a right not to sell to somebody whom you suspect of shady dealings. You might also want to refuse bids from buyers with lousy feedback profiles or with no feedback at all, but eBay does not explicitly say that this is allowed (the closest we could find was 'a seller may cancel the bid of any user with whom they would be uncomfortable completing a transaction'). At any rate, if you are only prepared to deal with bidders who fit a certain profile – at least 50 previous transactions with a positive feedback score of at least 98% and no previous bid retractions, for instance – then you should say so very clearly indeed in your item description.

Bid retraction is possible but don't do it too often, for each retraction is logged in your profile.

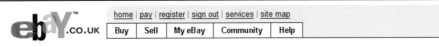

Bid Retractions:

Before bidding on an item on eBay, be sure to read the item description and check the seller's feedback. If you have any questions about the listing, contact the seller by going to the View Item page and clicking on either the seller's User ID or on the Ask Seller a Question link.

Please remember that every bid on eBay is binding (unless the item is listed in a category under the Non-Binding Bid Policy or the transaction is prohibited by law or by eBay's User Agreement). Bidding on multiple identical items should be done only if you intend to buy all of the items.

It is ONLY OK to retract a bid if...,

- ◆ You accidentally enter a wrong bid amount (for example, you bid £99.50 instead of £9.95). If this occurs, re-enter the correct bid amount immediately.
- ◆ The description of an item you have bid on has changed significantly.
- ◆ You cannot reach the seller. This means that you have tried calling the seller and the seller's phone number doesn't work, or you have tried emailing the seller and it comes back undeliverable.

Before you retract your bid, please read complete information on bid retractions including the Special Retraction Rules.

Item number of auction in question:

Making contact

If you want to talk to a buyer or a seller directly, you can ask eBay to supply their contact details. To do this, complete the Contact Info web form. To find the form, search the eBay help menu for keywords 'request contact information'.

You can only request contact details if you are currently involved in a transaction with that member or have been so involved recently, which means that one party must have bid on or won an auction hosted by the other party. Moreover, your request may be declined if the trader is located overseas. Perhaps most importantly, when eBay emails you the other party's contact details, it also emails your contact details – including the phone number you registered at the outset – to them.

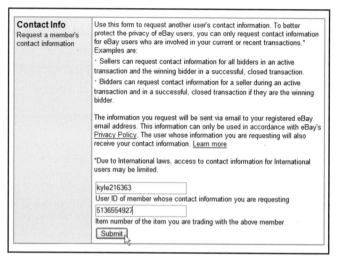

Most eBay communications take place with email but you can request a trader's phone number and address here.

Bidder blocking

You can stop any eBayer from bidding on your auctions. You might, for instance, want to have no further dealings with somebody who once left you unwarranted negative feedback, or who failed to pay promptly, or asked to deal privately outside of eBay, or who sent you spam email ... or whatever. It's entirely your choice.

To block a bidder, search the eBay Help menu for the keywords 'block bidder'. This will (eventually) take you to a form where you can enter the User IDs of people whom you wish to avoid. Any eBay member on this list will be unable to bid at your auctions.

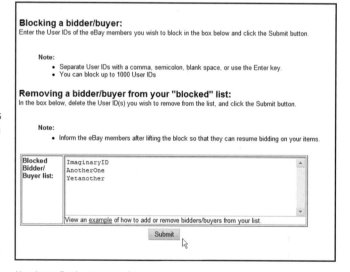

You have final say over who you are prepared to trade with – and who not.

PART  Accepting payment

My Robbie Williams CD auction runs to a close. It has
attracted 9 bids and sold for a less-than-whopping
£7.35. However, I set no reserve price so I am obliged to
sell. Before shipping the CD, I must get my money.
Here's how.

*As soon as the auction ends, I receive an email from
eBay confirming the closing price and the buyer's
details. At the same time, the buyer is sent an email
that confirms his purchase and includes payment
instructions. However, it is sound policy to also send the
buyer an invoice. To do this, open your My eBay page
and click the Sold link under All Selling in the sidebar.
Here you will find your item. Click Send Invoice*

*Click Send Invoice again in the following screen. This
opens a form in which you can specify the total postal
charges and add any comments. Check the Copy me
on this email to send yourself a copy of the invoice (this
is handy for your records). Click Send.*

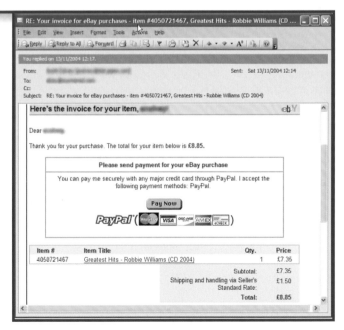

*The buyer then receives a formal invoice from eBay. If
PayPal is one of your payment options, or the only one,
the invoice will include a Pay Now button that links
directly to the buyer's PayPal account and prompts him
to pay the required amount.*

④

When payment is made, PayPal emails you immediate confirmation. You will now have cleared funds in your PayPal account and you should post the item straight away.

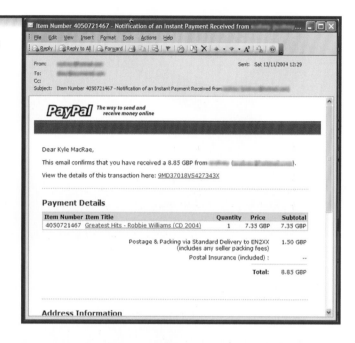

⑤

Log in to PayPal, click My Account, and click History. Here you will find details of your payment (including the fee deduction). If you want to leave the cash there to pay for future eBay auctions that you win, fine; if you want to transfer it to your bank account, click the Withdraw tab on this page and follow directions. Remember, it costs 25p to withdraw under £50.

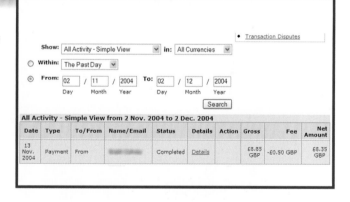

⑥

Back in eBay, you'll find a couple of reminders on the My Summary page. Return to the Sold auction details, as in Step 1, and click the button in the Action column. Select Mark Despatched to keep eBay and your own records up to date. At some point, ideally when the buyer has left positive feedback for you, return to this screen and select Leave Feedback in the Action column. As shown earlier, complete the web form and show your appreciation.

6

PART **6** eBay MANUAL

When it all goes horribly wrong

WHEN IT ALL GOES HORRIBLY WRONG

Covering your back

You may well be nervous about using eBay, and you would be right to be so. You simply don't have the same rights or protection that you do as a consumer shopping on the high street or even with a web-based retailer. Indeed, selling items can also be hit and miss.

For instance, let's say you win an auction, make payment ... and then nothing happens. Your goods don't arrive and the seller either ignores your emailed enquiries or fobs you off with stories about postal delays. If you or the seller paid for insurance, you may be able to make a claim and, if the seller is paranoid about his eBay reputation, he may offer a refund for fear of negative feedback. But he may just leave you stranded, out-of-pocket and item-less.

Or let's say you sell an item and the buyer claims non-delivery. Again, if you don't have insurance and you didn't use recorded delivery, what can you do? The buyer may threaten negative feedback unless you provide a refund ... and you may feel obliged to cough up.

However, you are not completely unprotected. Here's a summary of the options.

Credit card protection

If you use your credit card to pay for an item, you are automatically protected to a degree by your credit card company. For instance, if the goods don't arrive, you can process a 'chargeback' against the seller. It's a hassle – ask your card issuer for details – but it can be done, and it works. Essentially, the payment is credited back to your account and the credit card company seeks redress from the seller.

" No. Why should I give you my autograph? You'll only sell it on eBay! "

Incidentally, this is true even when you make a credit card payment through PayPal (which is why PayPal is so keen for you to pay for items via bank transfer rather than credit card – see Step 8 on p94). PayPal then has to reclaim the lost money from the seller – if it can.

PayPal Buyer Protection

If you use PayPal to pay for auctions, you may have automatic insurance against non-delivery or goods turning out to be 'significantly different than what was described in the listing' – but only under certain specific circumstances. These circumstances depend initially on the status of the seller, who must:

● Have received 50 or more eBay feedbacks.

● Have a positive feedback rating of 98% or higher.

● Be 'verified' with PayPal and have a Premier or Business account in the US, Canada or EU.

These conditions being met, you would see a PayPal Buyer Protection Offered logo next to the seller's User ID on the auction page (it appears automatically when a seller meets these criteria, no application is required).

As a buyer, you must be sure to:

● Use PayPal to pay for the item.

● Send payment to an email address linked to the seller's PayPal account (to ensure this, always use the Pay Now button when you receive a PayPal invoice, as Step 3 on p144).

These conditions also being met, you have 30 days from payment in which to file a claim with PayPal's Buyer Protection scheme. PayPal will investigate the case by talking to both parties and should meet the first £250 of any claim (recently increased to £500 but we're not sure if that's a permanent move). Only tangible goods are covered, not services, and you may make only two claims per year.

eBay Buyer Protection

If an auction does not qualify under the above terms – i.e. whenever the PayPal Buyer Protection Offered logo does *not* appear – then you may still be able to claim under eBay's own Standard Purchase Protection Programme. This covers claims of up to £120, less the first £15. Again, inevitably, there are limitations, among them these:

● You can only file a claim within 90 days but after 30 days.

● You must first file a complaint. This can be as early as 10 days after the auction ends.

● The item must have sold for over £15 excluding postage and other charges.

● You may make no more than three claims per six months.

● Items damaged or lost in transit are not covered.

● Items paid for with cash, money transfers or postal orders are not covered.

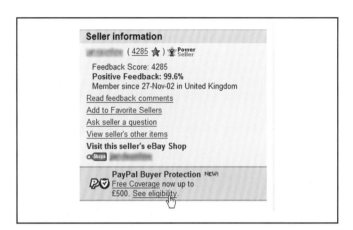

Look for the PayPal Buyer protection logo for a little peace of mind. The logo also appears next to eligible items in search results pages.

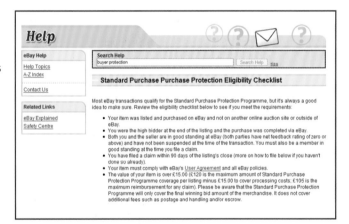

Get the lowdown on the complex Buyer Protection in the eBay Help system.

The clause excluding items 'lost in transit' is troublesome, because 'items never received' (in the sense of never sent) *are* covered. Here is eBay's take on it:

Items that are lost or damaged during transit are not eligible for eBay's Fraud Alert and Standard Purchase Protection Programme programmes unless you are the buyer AND one of the following conditions apply:

- You purchased postal insurance and the seller failed to insure the item.
- You purchased postal insurance and you or the seller filed a claim with the postal carrier, but the claim was denied due to poor packaging.
- You purchased postal insurance, you or the seller filed a claim with the postal carrier and the postal carrier awarded the seller reimbursement but the seller failed to send a refund to you.

In other words, you can only hope to claim for non-delivery if the item was insured during transit. Postal insurance is still a relative rarity in eBay auctions. The only other option is to file a complaint, or 'Fraud Alert', against the seller. If he says he shipped the item, you are effectively accusing him of lying.

The entire process is tortuous but in the end eBay will investigate your claim and, if it considers it just, reimburse you. Note that you cannot claim under both PayPal *and* eBay protection policies. For details, search eBay Help for the keywords 'buyer protection'.

Consumer protection

There is a further possibility of protection enshrined in the Consumer Protection (Distance Selling) Regulations Directive, 2000. This states that when a transaction takes place at a distance – i.e. where there is no face to face contact between buyer and seller – consumers have the right to return the item and get a refund for any reason whatsoever within a 7-day cooling off period following delivery. It is thus conceivable that you have an absolute right of return when you buy any item on eBay should it arrive damaged, not as you expected or even if you just change your mind. You may or may not be required to meet the return postage costs, depending on the terms of sale.

The Directive explicitly excludes internet auctions ... but is eBay an auction house? eBay itself says no and a German court recently upheld the interpretation that eBay traders are subject to the regulations. We do not believe it has yet been tested in the UK.

The Directive applies only to commercial traders, not to private individuals engaged in private transactions – but on eBay, what exactly is the difference? Should a distinction be drawn between new items and used items? And how about items sold as Buy It Now-only – surely that's as close to a regular distance commercial sale as it's possible to come?

These and other issue will doubtless be hammered out in the courts. If it turns out that bona fide eBay traders really *do* have to grant a 7-day cooling off period and right of return to all buyers, we suspect that we'll see some drastic changes in the way eBay operates.

9. An item that is 'dead on arrival' must be notified to us via email within 7 days of receipt of the item, for the item to be replaced.

10. In line with the current distance selling directive, all items have a 7 day money back guarantee, from the date of receipt of the item. In the event of the buyer wishing to return an item, postage costs are born by the sender and a RA (Returns Authorisation) number must be requested first by email

11. ████████ UK do not accept liability for any return costs nor do we accept responsibility for returns that are inadvertently lost should your selection of return method not allow you to track the item. You should ensure that the

Some – but not, we think, many – eBay traders are now offering an explicit cooling-off period in line with Distance Selling regulations.

Seller protection

Sellers have much less to worry about on eBay, primarily because you should only send the goods once you have received payment and, in the case of cheques, once that payment has cleared. If you send out an item before you have the cash, you're asking for trouble.

PayPal offers a Seller Protection policy but it's a minefield. The idea is that you are covered against fraudulent claims from buyers, including chargebacks, when you accept PayPal payments, but only on certain conditions. The main points are (or at least seem to be) these:

- You, the seller, must have a verified Premier or Business PayPal account.
- Claims for 'goods that are not as described' are excluded.
- UK sellers are eligible only when dealing with buyers based in the UK or US (for now at least).
- You must be able to provide proof of postage.
- If the item is worth over £150, you used a delivery service that requires a signature upon delivery.
- You must ship within seven days of payment.
- You must ship to the buyer's address listed in the Transaction Details page in PayPal.

Escrow

A big 'hmmmm' here. The idea with Escrow services is that a buyer pays money to a third-party rather than directly to a seller. Only when the buyer is happy with the goods does the seller get his money. The Escrow service charges a fee, buyer and seller are both protected, and everybody is happy.

Given that virtually all sellers refuse to ship goods until payment has cleared, Escrow is obviously more to the buyer's advantage than to the seller's. This is why you'll find precious few auctions flagged with Escrow as an optional extra (and remember, the seller always sets the terms). If Escrow is available, the buyer usually meets the bill (from around £15 upwards).

Until Escrow becomes much more common on eBay, it's really not an option for most auctions. However, our hunch is that Escrow in one form or another will come to prove central to eBay as the site expands. As scam artists multiply and become ever more devious and as more and more impatient newcomers undermine the value of feedback, it can only become harder to rely on the old values of community, trust and fair trading.

Meanwhile, Escrow is certainly attractive for high-value items, especially if it's impossible to arrange for first-hand inspection and collection. Check out **www.escrow.com** for details.

Not every transaction is eligible for PayPal's Seller Protection – but you only have the status confirmed after the event.

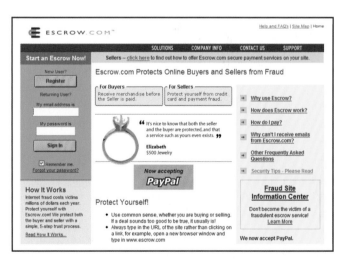

Escrow is worth considering where there's a lot of money at stake.

PART 6 Deadbeat buyers, re-listing and second-chance offers

If a winning bidder fails to pay, eBay will refund your final valuation fee i.e. the fee levied on a percentage of the selling price. Search the Help menu for keywords 'unpaid item policy' for full details and links to the relevant web forms. You can also re-list the item (but only within 90 days). If it sells second time around, eBay refunds the second insertion fee so effectively you get two bites at the cherry. If it doesn't sell, too bad: you have to pay the fee both times. If the item has a reserve price on its first outing, you can relist with the same or a lower reserve only; and if it didn't, you can't add a reserve now. In fact, you can use this option any time an item fails to sell, whether or not you are lumbered with a non-paying buyer and an Unpaid Item dispute.

You can also make a Second Chance Offer to the next highest bidder if the auction winner fails to pay up. Say somebody snipes an auction for £15.50, just beating a bid of £15.00, but then refuses to pay up (for whatever reason). You should certainly file an Unpaid Item claim but you can also offer the item to any beaten bidder for the price that they bid. In other words, you can offer to sell the item for £15 to the second highest bidder. You cannot ask anyone to pay more than their highest bid. If they are not interested, approach the next highest bidder and so on down the line.

You can even, surprisingly, offer an identical item to beaten bidders without having to list the item afresh. That is, you can legitimately approach anybody who lost out on an item and say, 'Too bad you didn't win the auction but if you're interested I have an identical item here which you can have for the value of your highest bid.'

eBay is happy with this arrangement because it charges a final value fee for each such sale; you might be happy because it saves you the bother of listing the second item. It also saves you the insertion fee plus whatever add-ons you paid for first time around.

To make a Second Chance Offer, open your My eBay page, find the item in the Sold section of All Selling, and use the button in the Action column to select Send a Second Chance Offer. You will then be shown a list of losing bidders. Select one or more and the rest is automatic. You must act within 60 days of the auction close.

Deadbeat buyer fails to cough up? You can either reclaim your final value fee and relist the auction, or offer it to the next highest bidder.

Second Chance Offer

To submit this offer, please select a duration and bidder below, then click **Continue**.

Original item number:	4050721467
Title:	Greatest Hits - Robbie Williams (CD 2004)
Duration:	1 day ▾

Select bidders who will receive your offer
The number of bidders you select can't be more than the number of duplicate items you have to sell. The Second Chance Offer price is a Buy It Now price determined by each bidder's maximum bid. Learn more

Select	User ID	Second Chance Offer Price
☑	░░░░░ (0)	£6.85
☐	░░░░░ (7)	£4.97
☐	░░░░░ (25 ☆)	£4.51
☐	░░░░░ (7)	£3.21
☐	░░░░░ (184 ☆)	£2.50

Bidders who have chosen not to receive Second Chance Offers or who have already been sent one will not appear above.

Receive a copy of your Second Chance Offer

☐	Send me a copy at ░░░░░
	Change my email address

WHEN IT ALL GOES HORRIBLY WRONG

Fraud and how to avoid it

eBay has long been a darling of the press – columnists and feature writers just can't resist talking about the football with which David Beckham missed a Euro 2004 penalty selling for £18,400 or repeating *ad infinitum* the story of how a decommissioned nuclear bunker fetched a cool £14,000 – but this enthusiasm has been tempered of late with stories of fraud. Nearly every week, it seems, some scam artist successfully cons people into paying for non-existent goods; and tales of PayPal users having their bank accounts fleeced are legion.

There's the triangulation scam, for instance. You win an auction for a new item, pay up and the item arrives. Fantastic, you think – until the police come looking for you and the item. What's happened here is that the seller has ordered the item from a mail order or internet retailer in your name and for delivery to your address, but used a stolen credit card. When the card is later reported stolen, the bank has a record of somebody – you, it seems – ordering the item from the supplier for home delivery. You end up under suspicion of having used a stolen credit card and your 'purchase' is promptly reclaimed. Meanwhile, the seller walks away with your money.

Should you be worried?

Yes, in a word. Or, more accurately, you should be cautious. Here are some guidelines:

● Research a seller's feedback thoroughly, read item descriptions carefully, ask the seller a question to resolve any doubts … and go with your instinct. If you suspect shady dealings, walk away at once. For instance, it's quite common to find an auction that seems to sell a specific item, such as an iPod, but in fact sells only information about how and where you can buy one cheaply. This 'information' commonly takes the form of a worthless link to a useless web page or buys you entry into a draw to, ahem, win the item. Avoid like the plague.

● Don't pay for items with cash in the mail or by a wire service like Western Union. Ever. In fact, if an auction insists on those methods of payment, don't even make a bid. These options allow the seller to obtain virtually untraceable cash payments, whereupon your chances of pursuing a claim for non-delivery or getting recompense in a triangulation scam are effectively zero.

● The safest option is to use your credit card for payment, whether through PayPal or directly with the seller (usually only possible where the seller runs an established business and not always even then). When you use your credit card, you should have automatic protection against fraud. Ask your card issuer for details.

- If a seller tries to change the terms of the deal after you've won an auction, refuse to comply. Do not pay higher shipping charges than were billed and do not agree to send cash if PayPal was listed as a payment option. A seller has no right to make such changes after the close and you have no obligation to agree to them.
- If it looks too good to be true, it is.

Spoof emails and 'phishing'

For our money, as it were, the most dangerous scam of all is 'phishing'. What typically happens here is that you receive an email purporting to be from PayPal. It looks like an official PayPal message, with the proper logo and everything, but it is nothing of the kind. The message will say something such as 'Click here to verify your account' or will explain that a system failure requires you to re-register or update your details. The trick is to persuade you to click a link in the email, which then opens a web page in your browser. This web page looks for all the world like a PayPal login screen but in reality it's just a clever spoof. Should you enter your user name and password, they will be grabbed by crooks who can then log into your PayPal account. From there, they can access, and potentially empty, your bank account.

eBay is sometimes targeted for a similar scam. If you allow your user name and password to fall into the wrong hands, it's possible for con artists to set up dummy auctions and 'sell' valuable items using your good name. They then pocket the money and ship no goods. First, though, they change the email address registered with eBay so that you don't receive any auction listing or sales confirmations.

Don't take the bait

It's a scary prospect indeed and many people have been thus conned. After all, eBay and PayPal send their users many emails and it's all too easy to click a link and think you're logging into the legitimate system. What we need are some golden rules:

● If an email asks you for your user ID and/or password – it may even contain fields in which you can enter these details directly – then it's a scam. eBay and PayPal *never* ask for these details by email. Indeed, eBay and PayPal will never ask you for your password under any circumstances.

● If an email asks you to click a link to log in to the service or to your account, be wary. This link may take you to a shadow site designed to look exactly like eBay or PayPal. To access your account, *always* do so via the site's home page – **www.ebay.co.uk** or **www.paypal.com/uk** – and always get to that page by typing the address into your browser or via a saved bookmark, never through a link in an email.
According to PayPal, PayPal will never send an email with the greeting 'Dear PayPal User' or 'Dear PayPal Member'. Real PayPal emails will address you by your first and last name or the business name associated with your PayPal account.
And according to eBay, eBay will never ask you to enter sensitive personal information such as User ID, password or bank account details directly by completing a form within the email or in an attachment. eBay will also never link you to a sign-in page where you will be asked to provide credit card or bank account details. This is a clear indicator of a spoof email.

● If you suspect that you have been sent a spoof email, report it to the site. You'll find links to the PayPal Security Centre and the eBay Safety Centre at the foot of their respective home pages. Or simply forward suspicious messages directly to **spoof@paypal.com** or **spoof@ebay.co.uk**.

● Never download an attachment sent with an eBay or PayPal message. This is another certain sign of a scam.

For more on spoof emails, go here:
http://pages.ebay.co.uk/education/spooftutorial/index.html

Never click a link in a suspicious email purporting to come from eBay or PayPal.

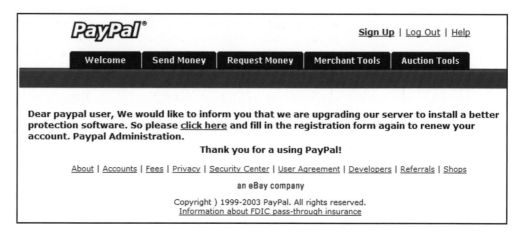

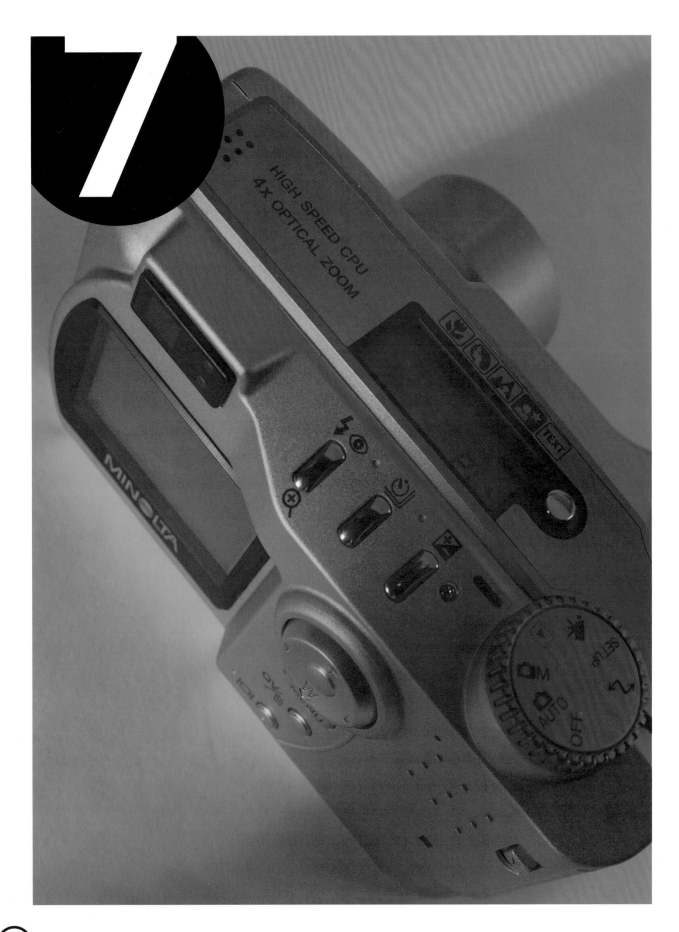

PART 7

eBay MANUAL

Appendices

Appendix 1 — Pictures

One of the trickiest aspects of selling on eBay is having
to provide pictures of your items. While not strictly
obligatory, pictures are generally expected. Obviously
there are many exceptions, such as concert tickets,
ringtones for mobile phones, anything that qualifies as a
service rather than as a tangible product, and so on.
Equally obviously, there's no pressing need to photograph
a new, sealed DVD or music CD when a stock photo (as
on p127-131) will suffice. But in general, bidders will
want to see at least one photograph of the actual item
that's up for auction.

Moreover, they rightly expect photographs to accurately depict
the true condition of the item. It's back to the trust and feedback
thing: you might be able to disguise a flaw by photographing an
item at a particular angle or shooting it just out of focus, but it
will come back to haunt you later when the buyer makes a claim
against you and blights your profile with negative feedback. Don't
take risks and don't try to hoodwink people.

We suspect you'd have to do
rather better than this to sell a
1927 Model T Ford.

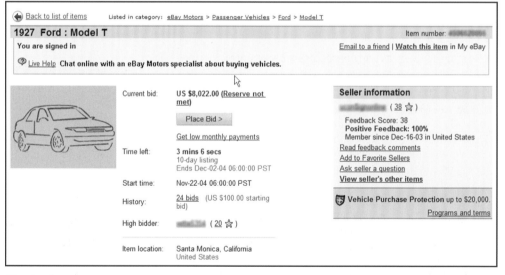

Techniques

So how should you go about showcasing your item to advantage?
Here are some ideas.

Digital camera By far the easiest approach. Take a snap, transfer
it from the camera to your computer's hard drive and upload it
directly to your auction listing with eBay's automatic picture
service (see p133). Always save your photos in the highly
compressed JPG (or JPEG) format. This keeps file sizes small,
and thus quick to upload and download, without overly
compromising image quality. In any case, eBay will convert non-
JPG images to the correct format during upload. It also crops

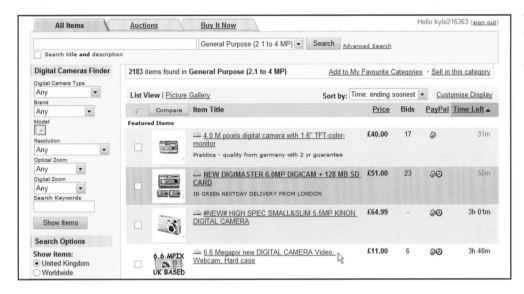

		All Items	Auctions	Buy It Now			Hello kyle216363 (sign out)	

You don't need to spend much to bag a basic digital camera that's more than adequate for snapping auction items.

them to 400 x 300 pixels so you might as well save them at this resolution in the first place.

Without labouring the point, your pictures should:

● Be in focus.

● Be in colour.

● Show the item accurately.

● Be cropped to remove any unnecessary background.

Scanner If your item is flatish, you may be able to scan it instead of taking a photograph.

Traditional camera If your only option is to take photographs with a film camera, either scan the prints or have your developer supply images in digital format on CD. But it's really very much easier to use a digital camera. You can pick one up for next to nothing on ... eBay.

Theft You can, if you like, copy a picture of an item from another website and claim it as your own. This is just about forgivable when you're selling a new or as-new item that exactly matches the picture. However, you should make it clear in your description that it's a 'stock' photo, not a photo of your actual item.

You can even copy a picture from another eBay auction where the same item is up for grabs – but you'll be in serious trouble if you get caught (and you will). eBayers don't take kindly to this kind of thing and you could find yourself reported for misconduct and potentially booted out of the community. Definitely something to avoid.

If you really can't provide your own photo, say so in the item description and explain why. By all means include a link to the relevant page on the manufacturer's website or to a retail site like Amazon to illustrate the general product, but be certain to mention any differences ('I'm selling the English-language version of this product') or damage ('Boxed and as new except for a tiny scuff mark').

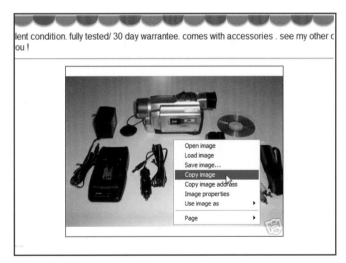

Picture theft from other auctions is easy on eBay. It is also very likely to get you into serious trouble. Don't do it.

Picture Service or DIY?

If you have your own web space, you can opt to 'host' your own images rather than uploading them to eBay. In this case, simply choose the 'Your own Web hosting' option when listing an item and enter the appropriate web address, or URL, that points directly to your picture (e.g. **www.mywebsite.co.uk/front_view.jpg**).

The trouble here is that you only get a chance to enter one URL whereas you might want to show several images of your item. The easy answer is merge several images together in a collage. This way, you get the benefit of multiple pictures without having to pay eBay's surcharges. Just be sure to keep the entire image within reasonable dimensions and file size or else your viewers will have to wait an age for it to download.

You can even have pictures appear directly on your item description page. To do this, you need to insert a line of HTML code:

<img src="www.mywebsite.co.uk/front_view.jpg">

Again, the URL should point directly to the picture, which normally means it will end with 'jpg'. The picture will then appear within the text of your description, located at the point where you enter the code. Unless you know enough HTML to control picture positions precisely – something that's beyond the scope of this book – we suggest putting the code on a separate line rather than attempting to 'wrap' text around images.

If you take this route, be sure to tick the box marked 'The description already includes a picture URL for my item'. If you do this, your item will have a little green camera item on search results pages, which tells eBayers that there are pictures available (and thus encourages them to click on your item and investigate it further).

Make the most of thumbnails

Also note the option to include a separate URL for a gallery picture. This is a thumbnail (miniature) image positioned next to the item title when it shows up in the search hits page or when browsing categories. If you use eBay's Picture Services, this thumbnail will always be a shrunken version of the first (or only) picture that you upload. But if you include a separate URL, you can control which image appears here. You might, for instance, zoom in on a detail.

Thumbnails are always displayed at a resolution of 64 x 64 pixels and eBay simply shrinks larger images to fit. Rectangular images are also cropped and padded with white space to make them square. To make the most of your gallery thumbnail, create your own pre-cropped and pre-sized 64 x 64 pixel image and link to it here.

In short, eBay provides an easy and useful tool for uploading one or more pictures of your item, but you can achieve considerably more – and achieve it considerably more cheaply (each additional image hosted by eBay costs 15p) – by hosting your own pictures. You can then employ a custom gallery thumbnail and pepper your item description with embedded pictures.

Host your own images to circumvent eBay's fees.

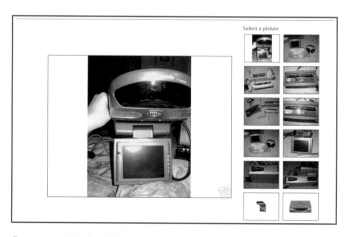

Buyers expect to be able to see what they're bidding on so don't skimp on the pictures.

Browsers and searchers can flit between list view and picture gallery view when looking for auctions. The latter option excludes all items that don't have thumbnails, which could put you at a disadvantage.

PART **7** # Appendix 2 – Setting up shop

We have looked exclusively at selling single items in this book because that is undoubtedly how you will begin to begin trading on eBay. But what if you want to take it further and turn a hobby into a business? Well, that's just what Simon and Audrey Jones did in 2004 with Handbags et al. Here we look at their story, in Simon's words.

Up and running

'We originally got started on eBay because we'd just got married and we needed some extra cash for Christmas. At first we sold all sorts of things from around the house, such as clothes, books, videos, and CDs. We made about £500 in one month which came in very useful at the time. Before this, we had discussed starting our own business so we could spend more time together. After selling all of our unwanted items on eBay, Audrey decided to look for something else to try and sell. This is where it gets tricky … buying and selling for a profit!

If you want to turn a hobby into a business, bag an online shop with an eBay storefront.

We decided that we would invest a small amount of money in some stock and see how it went. eBay very quickly became a full time business and within three months we had to concentrate on the business. It sounds like it all happened very quickly, and it did, but we were also very careful and did a lot of research!

We considered opening an eBay shop almost straight away after seeing our sample stock make a reasonable profit. One day, Audrey spent an hour or so fiddling with the eBay shop system and by the end of the day we had a rough shop up and running.

There are a number of advantages in having a shop within eBay. It is fairly cheap to do, so the cash investment risk is very limited, we get to have a unique web address (URL) which our regular customers can use to view *just our products* at any time, and it gives us a base for our marketing activities. It also helps eBay users recognise us as a legitimate and established business, helps us to build relationships with regular customers and gives our business an identity in a large and diverse market. Beyond that, the storefront system gives you access to a range of statistics and analysis created by eBay. These can be very useful when you know what you're looking for.

Having a specific URL means that our regular customers can bookmark us so they always know where to find us, and we have also set up a more traditional website – **www.handbagsetal.co.uk** – which links through to our eBay store.'

The eBay difference

Simon doesn't believe that there are any particular disadvantages to trading the eBay way but he does flag some important differences between running an eBay store and a traditional (online or offline) shop:

- eBay is a market in its own right. It is also predominantly auction-based so competition and current trends dictate the prices you will get for a product.

- People generally want a bargain on eBay and so are likely to pay less for your product than they would on the open market.

- eBay has its own set of rules and regulations which all sellers must obey.

- Fees are reasonable but do mount up when you are selling in quantity. But this is effectively your rent and you are only charged if something is sold so it's all relative.

- There is LOTS of competition!

And as for PayPal? Says Simon, 'We use PayPal as most people who use eBay recognise it as the quickest and most secure way to pay. We also accept cheques and postal orders but over 90% of our payments are made through PayPal.'

To see Simon and Audrey's online shop and get a feel for an eBay store, go to **www.stores.eBay.co.uk/handbagsetal**.

PART

Appendix 3 – A cynic's view

An item I ordered on eBay never arrived. I chased delivery after 14 days and was asked to give it more time. The item was being shipped to Europe from the US so this was a reasonable request. After 30 days, when it had still not arrived, the seller asked for my local post office details and said he would make a claim against his carriers. He then promised to send a new item. As I write, 16 days further on (i.e. 46 days from the sale) nothing has arrived. So what to do?

Let's assume that the item proves to be a no-show. Let's further assume, as seems likely, that the seller refuses to offer a refund. It is too late for me to make any claim on eBay or PayPal's protection policies, and the item was too cheap in any case. Basically, I have to write off my money. My only consolation is being able to leave appropriate feedback for the seller -- but herein lies the problem. I don't know whether the seller has been dishonest here or whether the postal service has let us both down (twice). For that matter, the seller may believe that I'm the one who's crooked, sitting here on two identical items and pretending that they never arrived. In any case, if I leave negative feedback he is sure to respond in kind. As it happens, the seller has received over 10,000 feedbacks and has a score of over 99%. My one negative feedback will make virtually zero difference to his reputation. However, having received only five positive feedbacks myself, a retaliatory negative feedback from the seller would thoroughly blight my profile. My positive feedback rating would then be a lousy 83.3% (five positives from a total of six feedbacks), which would effectively ruin my eBay career.

Upshot number one is that I dare not leave negative feedback even if I am convinced that I have been defrauded (I'm not thus convinced, but the point is that I might be and would still be scared to say so with feedback). Upshot number two is that seasoned eBayer sellers never leave feedback first, even when they receive immediate payment and courteous communications.

Leaving feedback first is a risky business. You can follow up an original comment if need be but you can't change a positive to a neutral or a negative.

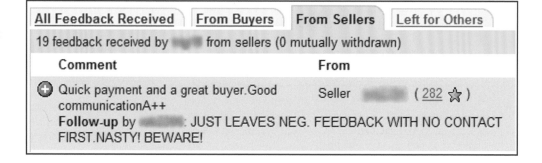

All Feedback Received	From Buyers	From Sellers	Left for Others

19 feedback received by ▓▓ from sellers (0 mutually withdrawn)

Comment	From
⊕ Quick payment and a great buyer.Good communicationA++	Seller ▓▓▓ (282 ☆)

Follow-up by ▓▓▓: JUST LEAVES NEG. FEEDBACK WITH NO CONTACT FIRST.NASTY! BEWARE!

This means that they always have the chance to hit back at a disgruntled buyer, however unfairly, which in turn discourages said buyer from being honest about his experience and thereby warning others.

The feedback system may provide the fabled trust upon which eBay is founded, but it's a flawed and fragile system.

The real cost of fraud?

How many deals go sour on eBay? Nobody knows for sure, partly because (for reasons just stated) a good deal probably go unreported for fear of feedback retaliation, and partly because overt fraud is hard to prove (items genuinely do get lost in the post). Some buyers fail to pay and the item gets quietly relisted without a fuss; other people doubtless get ripped off when buying questionable items but keep schtum rather than making a fuss. There are also degrees of fraud: you may consider that mis-describing an auction item is itself fraudulent, whereas others see this as part of the 'game'. At any rate, eBay's oft-quoted figure that fraud accounts for a mere 0.01% of transactions is, we suspect, wildly optimistic (and in any case only refers to 'confirmed' fraud). Curiously, there is no dedicated fraud discussion forum on eBay – because that would be to admit that the problem is real, perhaps? – but you'll find plenty of animated discussion sprinkled throughout the other Community Help Boards (**http://pages.ebay.co.uk/community/chat/index.html**).

For a name-and-shame antidote to rogue traders and a rundown of many major scams, check out eBayers That Suck at **www.ebayersthatsuck.com**.

Privacy concerns

On p82-83, we glance at the business of 'shadowing' another eBayer. On p143, we show you how to request somebody's phone number. Put these two together and what do you have?

- If you know somebody's eBay ID, you can find out which items they have bought recently and/or are bidding on currently.

- If you are already engaged in a transaction with this person, you can ask eBay for his telephone number. If you are not so engaged, all you have to do is bid on one of his auctions (assuming that he's selling something).

- eBay will also tell you in which town or city he is based.

- Armed with a telephone number, location and an eBay ID, you have a fairly good chance of identifying an individual, particularly if he has used a business telephone number (in which case an internet search will probably throw up the business name and address) and/or an ID that provides a clue to his name (like, er, my own 'kyle216363').

The potential here for embarrassment and even blackmail is, we trust, clear. To protect yourself, may we suggest that you register a non-traceable telephone number – you can get such a number from Yac (**www.yac.com**) – and choose an eBay ID that masks rather than reveals your real name.

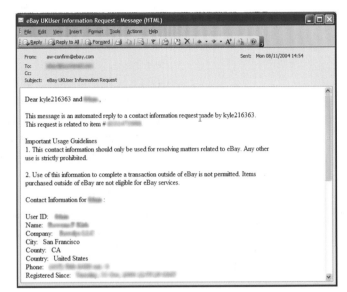

Ask for a trader's telephone number and you shall receive (so long as you are currently engaged in a transaction or have been so recently).

And so ...

eBay is constantly evolving and improving – the website is nowhere near as glitchy or unstable as once it was, for instance – but we believe it has a long way to go before a prospective buyer can feel truly confident. The existing protection policies are confusing and arguably inadequate, and we really wish there was a viable, popular and secure alternative to PayPal. EBay's willingness to divulge personal information on request is also concerning, particularly if you harboured any illusion that you could buy and sell in relative anonymity.

But for all that, eBay works ... most of the time ... if you keep your wits about you and develop a keen eye for sharp practice and rogue trading.

Index

r

re-listing 152
refreshing, auction information 101, 103
registration
    eBay 28–9
    PayPal 60–1
regulations *see* legalities
reserve prices 87–9, 121
    fees 122, 123
restricted goods/services 27
retracting bids 107, 138, 140–2
risks 22–3, 24
    see also feedback; fraud
rogue trading *see* fraud

s

saving searches 43–4
scanning items 159
scheduled listings 122, 130
searching 32–44
    advanced 35–44
    broadening searches 40–1, 42
    either/or expressions 40
    Favourites 43–4
    item titles 124
    location 43
    Matching Categories 42
    mis-spellings 43, 124
    narrowing 42
    phrases 41
    quotation marks 41
    within results 42
    saving searches 43–4
    spelling 43, 124
    subtitles 124
    widening searches 40–1, 42
    wild cards 40–1
    see also keywords
second chance offers 152
security 148–52
    see also fraud; protection
self-support system 25
sellers
    feedback 51–3
    other items 77
    protection 151
seller's guide 119–45
selling examples
    EAN items 127–31
    manual listing 132–5
shadowing 82–3, 102, 104
'shill' bidding 26
shipping 78, 80, 93, 96–7, 111, 120, 130
    see also delivery addresses
shop, setting up 161

signing up
    eBay 28–9
    PayPal 60–1
similar items, selling 136–7
sniping 13, 17, 90–1, 100–13
    group 111–13
    manual 100–5
    single items 108–10
    to win 106–13
sorting, auction information 37
spelling, searching 43, 124
starting prices 87–9, 121
stock photos 129, 158
stores, setting up shop 161
strategies, bidding 12–13, 17
sub-categories, listing items 128
subtitles
    fees 123
    searching 124
summaries
    bidding example 17
    bidding pitfalls 100
    feedback 49–50

tactics 23
telephone numbers, traders' 143, 163
thumbnails, pictures/photography 160
timing
    bidding 13, 23
    fixed 12–13, 19
    titles, item 124
tracking
    auctions 84–6, 136–43
    shadowing 82–3, 102, 104
trading, setting up shop 161
translation services 81
triangulation fraud 153–5
trust 24 – *see also* feedback; fraud

User Agreements
    eBay 26, 29
    PayPal 58
user forums 25, 31

valuations 120
verification, PayPal 66–7

watch list, My eBay 84–6, 108
widening searches 40–1, 42
wild cards, searching 40–1

ACKNOWLEDGEMENTS

Author	**Kyle MacRae**
Copy editor	**Sheena Deuchars**
Designer	**Lee Parsons**
Page build	**James Robertson**
Photography	**Simon Clay**
Project Manager	**Louise McIntyre**
Index	**Nigel d'Auvergne**